Praise for Johnny Townsend

In *Zombies for Jesus*, "Townsend isn't writing satire, but deeply emotional and revealing portraits of people who are, with a few exceptions, quite lovable."

Kel Munger, *Sacramento News and Review*

Townsend's stories are "a gay *Portnoy's Complaint* of Mormonism. Salacious, sweet, sad, insightful, insulting, religiously ethnic, quirky-faithful, and funny."

D. Michael Quinn, author of *The Mormon Hierarchy: Origins of Power*

Johnny Townsend is "an important voice in the Mormon community."

Stephen Carter, editor of *Sunstone* magazine

The Circumcision of God "asks questions that are not often asked out loud in Mormonism, and certainly not answered."

Jeff Laver, author of *Elder Petersen's Mission Memories*

"Told from a believably conversational first-person perspective, [*The Abominable Gayman*'s] novelistic focus on Anderson's journey to thoughtful self-acceptance allows for greater character development than often seen in short stories, which makes this well-paced work rich and satisfying, and one of Townsend's strongest. An extremely important contribution to the field of Mormon fiction." Named to Kirkus Reviews' Best of 2011.

Kirkus Reviews

"The thirteen stories in *Mormon Underwear* capture this struggle [between Mormonism and homosexuality] with humor, sadness, insight, and sometimes shocking details....*Mormon Underwear* provides compelling stories, literally from the inside-out."

Niki D'Andrea, *Phoenix New Times*

In *Sex among the Saints,* "Townsend writes with a deadpan wit and a supple, realistic prose that's full of psychological empathy....he takes his protagonists' moral struggles seriously and invests them with real emotional resonance."

Kirkus Reviews

"The Buzzard Tree," from *The Circumcision of God*, was a finalist for the 2007 Whitney Award for Best Short LDS Fiction.

"Townsend's lively writing style and engaging characters [in *Zombies for Jesus*] make for stories which force us to wake up, smell the (prohibited) coffee, and review our attitudes with regard to reading dogma so doggedly. These are tales which revel in the individual tics and quirks which make us human, Mormon or not, gay or not…"

A.J. Kirby, The Short Review

"The Rift," from *The Abominable Gayman*, is a "fascinating tale of an untenable situation…a *tour de force.*"

David Lenson, editor, *The Massachusetts Review*

"Pronouncing the Apostrophe," from *The Golem of Rabbi Loew*, is "quiet and revealing, an intriguing tale…"

Sima Rabinowitz, Literary Magazine Review, NewPages.com

The Circumcision of God is "a collection of short stories that consider the imperfect, silenced majority of Mormons, who may in fact be [the Church's] best hope.…[The book leaves] readers regretting the church's willingness to marginalize those who best exemplify its ideals: those who love fiercely despite all obstacles, who brave challenges at great personal risk and who always choose the hard, higher road."

Kirkus Reviews

"Johnny Townsend's...keen observations on the human condition come in many shapes and sizes...reflecting on both his Jewish and Mormon backgrounds as well as life in the vast and varied American gay community...His perspective is sometimes startling, sometimes hilarious, sometimes poignant, but always compassionate."

Gerald S. Argetsinger, Artistic Director of the Hill Cumorah Pageant (1990-96)

In *Mormon Fairy Tales*, Johnny Townsend displays "both a wicked sense of irony and a deep well of compassion."

Kel Munger, *Sacramento News and Review*

"*Selling the City of Enoch* exists at that awkward intersection where the LDS ideal meets the real world, and Townsend navigates his terrain with humor, insight, and pathos."

Donna Banta, author of *False Prophet*

The Golem of Rabbi Loew will prompt "gasps of outrage from conservative readers...a strong collection."

Kirkus Reviews

"That's one of the reasons why I found Johnny Townsend's new book *Mormon Fairy Tales* SO MUCH FUN!! Without fretting about what the theology is supposed to be if it were pinned down, Townsend takes you on a voyage to explore the rich-but-undertapped imagination of Mormonism. I loved his portrait of spirit prison! He really nailed it—not in an official doctrine sort of way, but in a sort of 'if you know Mormonism, you know this is what it must be like' way—and what a prison it is!"

C. L. Hanson, *Main Street Plaza*

Zombies for Jesus is "eerie, erotic, and magical."

Publishers Weekly

"While [Townsend's] many touching vignettes draw deeply from Mormon mythology, history, spirituality and culture, [*Mormon Fairy Tales*] is neither a gaudy act of proselytism nor angry protest literature from an ex-believer. Like all good fiction, his stories are simply about the joys, the hopes and the sorrows of people."

Kirkus Reviews

"In *Let the Faggots Burn* author Johnny Townsend restores this tragic event [the UpStairs Lounge fire] to its proper place in LGBT history and reminds us that the victims of the blaze were not just 'statistics,' but real people with real lives, families, and friends."

Jesse Monteagudo, The Bilerico Project

Let the Faggots Burn: The UpStairs Lounge Fire is "a gripping account of all the horrors that transpired that night, as well as a respectful remembrance of the victims."

Terry Firma, Patheos

In *Let the Faggots Burn*, "Townsend's heart-rending descriptions of the victims…seem to [make them] come alive once more."

Kit Van Cleave, *OutSmart Magazine*

Marginal Mormons is "an irreverent, honest look at life outside the mainstream Mormon Church….Throughout his musings on sin and forgiveness, Townsend beautifully demonstrates his characters' internal, perhaps irreconcilable struggles….Rather than anger and disdain, he offers an honest portrayal of people searching for meaning and community in their lives, regardless of their life choices or secrets." Named to Kirkus Reviews' Best of 2012.

Kirkus Reviews

"The Sneakover Prince" from *God's Gargoyles* is "one of the most sweet and romantic stor[ies] I have ever read."

Elisa Rolle, Reviews and Ramblings, founder of The Rainbow Awards

"*Let the Faggots Burn* is a one-of-a-kind piece of history. Without Townsend's diligence and devotion, many details would've been lost forever. With his tremendous foresight and tenacious research, Townsend put a face on this tragedy at a time when few people would talk about it....Through Townsend's vivid writing, you will sense what it must've been like in those final moments as the fire ripped through the UpStairs Lounge. *Let the Faggots Burn* is a chilling and insightful glimpse into a largely forgotten and ignored chapter of LGBT history."

Robert Camina, writer and producer of the documentary *Raid of the Rainbow Lounge*

"Johnny Townsend's 'Partying with St. Roch' [in the anthology *Latter-Gay Saints*] tells a beautiful, haunting tale."

Kent Brintnall, Out in Print: Queer Book Reviews

Gayrabian Nights is "an allegorical tour de force...a hard-core emotional punch."

Gay. Guy. Reading and Friends

The stories in *The Mormon Victorian Society* "register the new openness and confidence of gay life in the age of same-sex marriage....What hasn't changed is Townsend's wry, conversational prose, his subtle evocations of character and social dynamics, and his deadpan humor. His warm empathy still glows in this intimate yet clear-eyed engagement with

Mormon theology and folkways. Funny, shrewd and finely wrought dissections of the awkward contradictions—and surprising harmonies—between conscience and desire." Named to Kirkus Reviews' Best of 2013.

Kirkus Reviews

"This collection of short stories [*The Mormon Victorian Society*] featuring gay Mormon characters slammed [me] in the face from the first page, wrestled my heart and mind to the floor, and left me panting and wanting more by the end. Johnny Townsend has created so many memorable characters in such few pages. I went weeks thinking about this book. It truly touched me."

Tom Webb, judge for The Rainbow Awards (A Bear on Books)

"The struggles and solutions of the individuals [in *Latter-Gay Saints*] will resonate across faith traditions and help readers better understand the cost of excluding gay members from full religious participation."

Publishers Weekly

Dragons of the Book of Mormon is an "entertaining collection....Townsend's prose is sharp, clear, and easy to read, and his characters are well rendered..."

Publishers Weekly

"The pre-eminent documenter of alternative Mormon lifestyles...Townsend has a deep understanding of his characters, and his limpid prose, dry humor and well-grounded (occasionally magical) realism make their spiritual conundrums both compelling and entertaining. [*Dragons of the Book of Mormon* is] [a]nother of Townsend's critical but affectionate and absorbing tours of Mormon discontent." Named to Kirkus Reviews' Best of 2014.

Kirkus Reviews

"Mormon Movie Marathon," from *Selling the City of Enoch*, "is funny, constructively critical, but also sad because the desire...for belonging is so palpable."

Levi S. Peterson, author of *The Backslider* and *The Canyons of Grace*

In *Gayrabian Nights*, "Townsend's prose is always limpid and evocative, and...he finds real drama and emotional depth in the most ordinary of lives."

Kirkus Reviews

Selling the City of Enoch is "sharply intelligent...pleasingly complex...The stories are full of...doubters, but there's no vindictiveness in these pages; the characters continuously poke holes in Mormonism's more extravagant absurdities, but they take very little pleasure in doing so....Many of Townsend's stories...have a provocative edge to them, but this [book] displays a great deal of insight as well…a playful, biting and surprisingly warm collection."

Kirkus Reviews

"Among the most captivating of the prose [in *Off the Rocks*, in a piece reprinted from the collection *A Day at the Temple*] was a story by Johnny Townsend illustrating two Mormon missionaries who break the rules of their teachings to spend more time with one another."

Lauren Childers, *Windy City Times*

Gayrabian Nights is a "complex revelation of how seriously soul damaging the denial of the true self can be."

Ryan Rhodes, author of *Free Electricity*

Gayrabian Nights "was easily the most original book I've read all year. Funny, touching, topical, and thoroughly enjoyable."

Rainbow Awards

Lying for the Lord is "one of the most gripping books that I've picked up for quite a while. I love the author's writing style, alternately cynical, humorous, biting, scathing, poignant, and touching…. This is the third book of his that I've read, and all are equally engaging. These are stories that need to be told, and the author does it in just the right way."

Heidi Alsop, Ex-Mormon Foundation Board Member

"If you like short stories and you're interested in the lives of Mormons, you should be following the work of Johnny Townsend. Since he writes from an ex-Mormon perspective, believers often dismiss Townsend's work as biased—or as *a priori* 'an attack on the church'—but I think that's a mistake. Johnny Townsend writes his characters with a great deal of compassion and empathy, whether they're in the church or not…or somewhere in between."

C. L. Hanson, *Main Street Plaza*

"Townsend is a wonderful writer with a wry but sympathetic eye for humans' frailties, and the ways in which religious belief both exacerbate and console them. [*Despots of Deseret* contains] more vibrant parables about doubts and blasphemies that hide beneath a veneer of piety." Named to Kirkus Reviews' Best of 2015.

Kirkus Reviews

In *Lying for the Lord*, Townsend "gets under the skin of his characters to reveal their complexity and conflicts….shrewd, evocative [and] wryly humorous."

Kirkus Reviews

In *Missionaries Make the Best Companions*, "the author treats the clash between religious dogma and liberal humanism with vivid realism, sly humor, and subtle feeling as his characters try to figure out their true missions in life. Another of Townsend's rich dissections of Mormon failures and uncertainties…" Named to Kirkus Reviews' Best of 2015.

Kirkus Reviews

In *Invasion of the Spirit Snatchers*, "Townsend, a confident and practiced storyteller, skewers the hypocrisies and eccentricities of his characters with precision and affection. The outlandish framing narrative is the most consistent source of shock and humor, but the stories do much to ground the reader in the world—or former world—of the characters….A funny, charming tale about a group of Mormons facing the end of the world."

Kirkus Reviews

Townsend's "works are on a cutting edge of history."

Walter Jones, Assistant Head of Special
Collections, Marriott Library

The Washing of Brains has "A lovely writing style, and each story was full of unique, engaging characters….immensely entertaining."

Rainbow Awards

"Townsend's collection [*The Washing of Brains*] once again displays his limpid, naturalistic prose, skillful narrative chops, and his subtle insights into psychology...Well-crafted dispatches on the clash between religion and self-fulfillment..."

Kirkus Reviews

The Last Days Linger was awarded Second Place for Best Gay Contemporary General Fiction in the 2017 Rainbow Awards

"While the author is generally at his best when working as a satirist, there are some fine, understated touches in these tales [*The Last Days Linger*] that will likely affect readers in subtle ways....readers should come away impressed by the deep empathy he shows for all his characters—even the homophobic ones."

Kirkus Reviews

In *Dead Mankind Walking*, "Townsend writes in an energetic prose that balances crankiness and humor....A rambunctious volume of short, well-crafted essays..."

Kirkus Reviews

What Would Anne Frank Do?

Making Humane Decisions

in a Time of Crisis

Johnny Townsend

BookLocker

Saint Petersburg, Florida

Published by BookLocker.com, Inc., St. Petersburg, Florida, U.S.A.

Printed on acid-free paper.

BookLocker.com, Inc.

2020

First Edition

Cover design by Todd Engel

For every worker, leader, civil servant, protester, activist, and volunteer taking risks to help others

Special thanks to Donna Banta

for her editorial assistance

For more of Donna's own work,

please read *False Prophet.*

Contents

Introduction:
What Would Anne Frank Do?

When faced with a moral decision, Christians often ask themselves, "What would Jesus do?" Atheists sometimes pose the same question by quoting Christ's actual words when they feel the secular answer is more "Christian" than the mainstream religious response. The problem is that some people think Jesus would rip children away from their parents and imprison them. Others think Jesus would make sure everyone was fed, with no effort to shame the hungry in the process. Some feel that Jesus would bomb civilians. Others don't believe Jesus would be the strongest supporter of waterboarding. It's clear there are far too many answers to this question for it to be useful as a tool in guiding our behavior.

So I decided to ask myself a different one.

As a Mormon, I considered, "What would Joseph Smith do?" But even the most basic awareness of the history behind the mythology steered me away from that litmus test pretty quickly. I *didn't* want to have sex with the family babysitter in the barn.

I next considered, "What would Gandhi do?" but that possibility was ruined as well when a former bank manager told me, "We should all be like Gandhi and help people get loans."

Perhaps then it's impossible to pose the question using any historical or religious figure. But I still felt the need for a moral template and decided to give "What would Anne Frank do?" a try.

Well, Anne Frank would record everything she witnessed, wouldn't she? She'd think, she'd revise to improve the accuracy and readability of her account, she'd make the best of a bad situation and try to see the good in people.

Still, Anne Frank could be a bit of a brat, to judge by her own writings.

Martin Luther King, Jr. had lots of extramarital sex.

Laura Ingalls Wilder was biased against Native Americans.

I began wondering if perhaps we should become "cafeteria" admirers and simply pick and choose which behaviors we wanted to emulate in others. But what kind of evaluation technique could I use to help me answer that?

"What would Jesus pick and choose?"

Dagnabbit!

We've been told it isn't good to meet our heroes, that the reality always falls short of the ideal. But there's no reason we can't appreciate the good in people and follow their positive examples without condoning their sins and failures. We can ask, "What would my mother do in this situation? What would Maria's grandfather do, Levi's high school English teacher, my neighbor Cathy's ex?" and take the best examples from everyone we know when making our own decisions on difficult matters.

One evening many years ago, while walking through the French Quarter, a friend and I heard the sound of scuffling from the block ahead, and a young woman's voice calling out desperately. "Help us! Help!"

My walking companion turned the corner and headed away from the mugging. And I followed, leaving the young couple to their fate.

Far too often, we follow the *worst* aspects of other people's behavior.

Still, if I wasn't brave enough to offer assistance on my own, why didn't I at least run into a bar and call the police?

If we find ourselves more flawed than Maya Angelou, or Rabbi Akiva, or Sarah Winnemucca, we need a Plan B.

Before the pandemic, my husband Gary went door to door once a month talking to people about socialism. My friend Robert volunteered to teach English to immigrant adults. My friend Donna volunteered at a public garden. Those are all great things, but I know myself well enough to understand I simply won't do them, even if things ever "return to normal." Yet there's no value beating myself up over it. I did manage to volunteer through Jewish Family Services to play pool regularly with an elderly shut-in. I volunteered as a proofreader for a progressive Mormon magazine and a socialist newspaper. I volunteered to help prepare meals for people with HIV. I volunteered a year and a half of my time researching the Upstairs Lounge fire. I volunteered as a slush pile reader for a science fiction magazine.

And I volunteer now by writing op-eds, taking part in a community effort to find solutions to our country's most pressing problems.

We can ask what our heroes, our mentors, our friends and family, would do in any given situation, but even if *they* would make an especially good decision regarding the question at hand, it's still not necessarily what *we* should do. Or even *can* do. I'm *not* going to call prospective voters on the phone even to support causes or candidates I believe in deeply. It's not that calling folks wouldn't be the right thing, it's simply that I won't do it, so I have to find something good I *will* do.

I get so tired of seeing successful CEOs or other people in prominent positions dismiss the needs of others with, "If I can do it, so can they." No, not everyone can be a CEO. And how, exactly, would society even function in this lift-yourself-up-by-your-bootstraps scenario? All CEOs and no workers? All management and no inventors or delivery drivers or physicians or plumbers?

We can't all perform the exact same high-paying—or low-paying—job. And we can't all make the exact same decisions when faced with a moral dilemma. What we can do, though, is choose a morally appropriate response out of the several possibilities before us.

I do a decent job of listening when someone wants to tell me what they're going through. I may not have anything useful to say in response, but sometimes the help is in not saying anything at all. I can't donate $10,000 to a good cause, but I can donate $15. I may never be the world's best author, but I can say a few things in a way that's meaningful to at least some people. I can keep my mind open to other opportunities that utilize my strengths. I can choose which weaknesses to work on and when.

There's no reason we can't consider what Theodora would do in our place, what the Buddha would do, what the Gaon of Vilna would do.

These are all fair questions and could very well provide useful guidance. Reflecting on the best course of action is almost always a good idea. Ultimately, though, the only question any of us can realistically ask ourselves is this: "What will *I* look back on—the last day of my life, with my life flashing before my eyes—and wish *I* had done?"

Let's Stop Digging Our Own Graves

(published in the *Salt Lake Tribune* on 21 February 2020)

A Canadian friend of mine complained that indigenous First Nations people kept refusing the jobs and industry offered them, insisting on government "handouts" instead. They should just "get over" their past abuse, he said, assimilate, and get on with life. My follow-up question was, "What kind of jobs and industry are we talking about?" Most of the industry I see on indigenous lands supports fracking and tar sands operations. Accepting such a job, no matter the salary, is like getting paid to dig your own grave.

We all know about the billions of gallons of water permanently contaminated by fracking. In a climate increasingly plagued by drought, that's no small matter. Most of the toxic chemicals are supposedly injected deep below ground to avoid polluting our drinking water, but the act of injecting water itself is directly responsible for the marked increase in earthquakes as large as 5.8 in every region where fracking takes place. And much of this "safe" drinking water is easily ignitable as it issues from residential taps.

Toxic water and damaging earthquakes aside, carbon-based fuels are the driving force behind the climate crisis. Driving faster is like thinking the solution to creating safer roadways is to speed when you see the stoplight turn yellow. Fracking also significantly increases emissions of methane, an even more potent greenhouse gas than carbon dioxide.

During World War II, Japanese soldiers often forced Filipino and American prisoners to dig their own graves. In Jim Crow times, white mobs sometimes committed this same atrocity against their black neighbors. Nazis not only forced many Jewish victims to dig their own graves, but they also forced black Allied POWs—and gays and Roma—to do so as well. Today, ISIS forces some of its victims to dig their own graves, too. It's a popular war crime.

Why would anyone agree to dig their own grave? They *know* what's going to happen when they finish. Why would they agree both to the hard work and the extreme humiliation? Why would they *help* their oppressors murder them?

People do it to buy time. Not time to be rescued. They know that won't happen. And not quality time. They get only a few awful, miserable minutes. But they are minutes of life.

So people of almost every culture, of every socioeconomic level, in conflict after conflict, agree to dig their own graves.

But some indigenous First Nations people refuse to take part in drilling. They and other activists pile barricades on railroad tracks to stop coal trains. Native Americans and other environmentalists are blocking pipeline construction in the Dakotas. Members of the Puyallup tribe are fighting a liquified natural gas facility in Washington state. Navajo and other concerned Utahns are fighting to prevent mining and drilling on public lands. Still other Utahns are fighting Salt Lake's inland port for aiding the transportation of fossil fuels.

These folks often suffer poverty as a result. They are routinely imprisoned for protesting.

But they don't dig their own graves.

In her Emmy acceptance speech, actress Alex Borstein spoke of her grandmother being led to a pit where she would be shot and dumped along with other Jews during the Holocaust. The woman turned to her guard and asked, "What happens if I step out of line?"

The guard assured her that although he wouldn't have the heart to shoot her, someone else would.

Borstein's grandmother stepped out of line. She survived while everyone else in the group was murdered. "So step out of line, ladies," the actress told the crowd. "Step out of line."

We don't have to accept fracking and oil wells and pipelines. We don't have to dig our own graves, even if we're being paid well to do the job. And we certainly don't have to accept being shamed for choosing life over death.

Corporations driving the climate crisis have forced us all into a global catastrophe. We're scared. We're hungry. Our kids need shelter.

But they don't need the shelter provided by a tombstone or a vault. If it's an atrocity to make us dig our own graves, it's unconscionable to force us to dig those of our children.

We must refuse all new fossil fuel extraction, storage, and transport. We must step out of line if we want a fighting chance at life.

It's Risky to Nominate a Democratic Socialist: It's Also Risky Not To

(published in *LA Progressive* on 14 February 2020)

Every day, pundits worry that it would be risky to nominate a Democratic Socialist to run in the general presidential election. They are 100% right. What they fail to note, of course, is that it's also risky to run a centrist. *Any* Democratic nominee is going to face an uphill battle. So let's choose the candidate with the best policies and fight as hard as we can to elect that candidate.

In 2016, Democrats *did* nominate a moderate. It didn't go so well. If people want to blame progressives or the Green Party or Putin or the Electoral College or anything else, the fact remains that every type of election interference from four years ago still exists today.

What if we nominate Warren? Trump and the GOP will attack her for having "claimed to be an Indian." What if we nominate Klobuchar? The attack will be that she's an "activist lawyer" or, conversely, that she prosecuted innocent black defendants.

Biden is "low energy" and sometimes stutters. No matter how inappropriate it is to mock him for his occasional trouble speaking, a president who mocks disabled reporters and POWs won't have any problem doing so. Will it subconsciously diminish Biden in the minds of voters? We don't know. But it's risky. And it's hardly Biden's only weak spot.

Buttigieg is gay. Would Trump suggest that having a First Gentleman would make the U.S. look bad? Of course he would. Just as he'd complain about Bloomberg "buying the election." Or Steyer having no experience in office. Pundits seem to have missed that Trump is a hypocrite *and* that his hypocrisy means little to his supporters. He'll use a Pee Wee Herman "I know you are but what am I?" attack on any opponent, no matter how ridiculous it looks to rational Democrats. And that approach works for him. Have we not been paying attention?

It wasn't just centrist Hillary Clinton who lost a bid for the presidency. Al Gore lost, too. So did Walter Mondale. And Adlai Stevenson. And John Kerry. And Michael Dukakis. And more. Yes, sometimes running a centrist is a winning strategy. But sometimes, it's not. It's risky. Just like running a Democratic Socialist.

The question is whether it's easier to rally a potential voter behind "We will guarantee you healthcare and a college education and a living wage" or "We can't really give you anything you need, but we can get rid of Trump."

Get rid of Trump! Yes! We want that!

But it's a false dilemma. A centrist can't guarantee he or she can win against Trump any more than a Democratic Socialist can. If it was guaranteed, we wouldn't need the election in the first place. It's risky to choose *either* option. So we must add other factors to our decision. And those other factors *must* include policy proposals.

Would Republicans have a hard time working with a Democratic Socialist? Undoubtedly. But are we under any illusion they'll eagerly work with *any* other Democratic president? If I remember correctly, GOP lawmakers weren't all that keen to work with Obama.

If a centrist's only significant argument is that they'll stop the country from deteriorating further under Trump, it's also true that a Democratic Socialist will do the same. We get that from either type of nominee.

If the stakes are so high that we need to go with the safest bet, the bland status quo of past centrists is hardly justifiable as that safe wager. We are in a time of crisis. Even without Trump in office, economic inequality has been growing for decades. Americans have come to understand that universal healthcare, something guaranteed in the rest of the industrialized world, is a right. What's risky is ignoring the tangible, physical needs of the people casting their ballots.

Most voters believe the science proving the climate emergency. They aren't going to be pacified with candidates who accept donations from fossil fuel corporations. A promise to "gradually" and "pragmatically" approach a crisis the majority understand must be addressed immediately is more than risky. It's foolhardy.

I want a woman president. I also want a Latino. And an Asian. One black president was hardly enough. I'd also like a Jew. And maybe an atheist. As a gay man, I'd certainly like to see a gay president.

But what we need more than any of that is a candidate with policies that will help us all. Medicare for All isn't negotiable. Neither is tuition-free college or vocational training. Or a Green New Deal. *Polls show that the majority of voters want these things.*

If it's a purity test to demand that a candidate support a woman's right to choose, we as an electorate have the right to demand other non-negotiables as well.

Is that risky? Of course it is. But it's even riskier not to.

COVID-19 Isn't My First Pandemic

(published in the *Seattle Times* on 6 March 2020)

I'm 58 and overweight, with diabetes and high cholesterol. This puts me in a high-risk category for COVID-19. But even those in the most vulnerable populations still have a 90% chance of survival. If we get the virus at all. Having lived through the AIDS crisis of the 1980's and 90's, where the mortality rate was close to 100%, I'm not particularly worried. As a character in one of my favorite 1980's movies, *Tootsie*, said, "Don't-don't-don't-don't panic."

Virtually every gay man my age has lost multiple friends and lovers. In our twenties and thirties, we checked the obituaries in the newspaper every morning. We watched friend after friend go blind, or develop dementia, or grow lesions, and die slow, miserable deaths. Death was a daily part of our life for years. But we went to work, we asked guys out on dates, we went to funerals, and we kept on living.

The Seattle Art Museum recently housed a special collection from the Capodimonte Museum in Naples. Having worked as a Mormon missionary in central and southern Italy, I wanted to experience part of that life again. In addition to the spectacular artwork, I was intrigued by a notecard accompanying one of the paintings. It mentioned that between 1656 and 1658, the bubonic plague wiped out almost 60% of Naples, nearly 150,000 people.

And you know what? The city survived.

In all, the bubonic plague wiped out roughly a third of the world's population in the Middle Ages and in later outbreaks. But life went on.

My grandfather caught the "Spanish flu" in 1918 and was deathly ill for several days. But he survived.

It's societal disruption that will be the larger issue. A native New Orleanian, my life was upended by Hurricane Katrina. Cell phones and the internet were down for weeks. Electricity was out for over a month in most places, sometimes several months. Pumps at gas stations don't work if there's no electricity. Washing machines don't work, either, and when you're cleaning up debris in 95-degree weather, you want to be able to wash your clothes.

A coworker in New Orleans committed suicide after losing everything. I never saw some of my friends again. I lost most of my belongings. I lost my job. I was forced to relocate thousands of miles away and start over. But you know what? I did. Life went on.

Panic will be an even larger issue. At the height of the AIDS crisis, people who were merely suspected of being gay, much less of having the virus, were fired from their jobs. They were kicked out of their apartments with no warning, their belongings dumped on the street.

When I told my grandmother, a rural Mississippi farmer, that I was gay, she wrote to her senators asking them to support gay rights. But she was afraid to hug me.

Disease has swept through human populations for millennia and will continue to do so as long as our species continues to share the planet with bacteria and viruses. Which means for the rest of human existence.

So let's take precautions. Let's wash our hands. Let's cover our coughs and sneezes. Let's stay home from work if we're sick. Let's push for universal healthcare, since the health of the poor and uninsured affects the health of everyone else, too. And the poor and uninsured deserve a fighting chance at life regardless, even apart from pandemics.

It's awful to be sick. And it's heartbreaking to lose loved ones. That's going to happen, though, regardless of COVID-19. My mother died of leukemia at 43. My husband died of liver cancer. A friend was stabbed to death by a gay basher. Premature death of any kind is genuinely tragic. But let's calm down and realize most of us will get through this.

I've already lived through a global pandemic. So have most of you. Let's take a deep breath and remember that the overwhelming majority of us will do so again. And again. And again.

Give a Man a Check…

(published in *LA Progressive* on 18 May 2020)

We've all heard the saying, "Give a man a fish, feed him for a day. Teach a man to fish and feed him for a lifetime." Helping someone care for their own needs rather than just offering a handout is clearly the better approach. And yet many on the right feel that *any* taxpayer-funded program that helps people take care of themselves is somehow instead hurting them. One of my former missionary colleagues describes most of this "purported" aid as "giving someone a check," insisting that the only thing it accomplishes is to make the recipient feel both entitled and dependent. Perhaps we should rephrase the left's approach in a more relatable way. "Give people a check, pay their bills for a month. Teach people job skills and let them pay their own bills for life."

If the U.S. could offer its citizens tuition-free college and vocational training, as many other nations do, no student need get "a check" at all. Students instead gain access to classrooms and teachers. They gain access to information, tutoring, labs, and fieldwork. They gain access to job and career competency so they can succeed in the workplace and provide for themselves and their families. This means a reduction in demand for taxpayer dollars directed to food assistance or subsidized housing. A reduction in demand for funds directed to jails and prisons filled with those spurred to find "alternate" methods of employment.

If the U.S. could offer its citizens genuine socialized healthcare, lowering the cost of drugs and medical supplies as an essential ingredient, as a nation we'd spend far less on healthcare than we do now. Those are funds that can be spent on consumer goods, on renewable energy research, on roads and bridges. With guaranteed healthcare (and guaranteed sick leave), fewer workers would need to come to work sick, spreading their cold or flu or COVID. There would be less absenteeism, more productivity. No one will be "giving a check" to someone to see a doctor, with the accompanying suspicion the recipient might run off to the race track instead. The ill person simply gets to seek medical care without having to worry about not having enough of his or her own funds left over to pay the light bill.

"But if we just let people get all the education they want and all the healthcare they need, they'll be spoiled brats. They won't appreciate how good they have it."

To be fair, that's a real possibility. But right now, the privileged children of rich parents get a good education and all the medical care they want, and no one seems to mind. There are no laws forcing all college students to pay their own way without any assistance from their parents or from scholarships or grants, forcing everyone over eighteen off their parents' insurance. Why are those on the right only worried about the gratitude of the masses? If getting an education without groveling is good enough for children of the wealthy, why do the rest of us have to clean toilets eight hours every night for the same privilege?

Why is it so, so important for peasants never to forget their place?

So they won't dare to rise out of it?

The truth is that students from low-income areas almost never receive the early education they need to succeed in college, even if they do manage to find a job that will allow them to earn the application fee. Adult children of the moneyed elite often turn out to be pretty awful human beings, but it's only the grown kids of the poor that we like to label "losers." If "giving someone a check" is so destructive to the poor, we'd have to believe that *not* helping them has proven a well-traveled path to virtue. And yet we've been judging and condemning these folks all of our lives for their moral failings.

Since *not* providing a good education hasn't worked either to improve the character of the poor *or* allow them skills to provide for themselves, maybe we've chosen a different motto altogether than the one we've enshrined. "Don't give a man a fish, starve him for a day. Refuse to teach him how to fish and starve him for a lifetime."

It's not as if folks who can't afford tuition are asking for honorary degrees.

Those on the right often demand that recipients of government assistance be working to qualify. And then make it almost impossible for the unskilled to get a job, especially when the job pays such low wages they can't even earn enough to cover childcare while they're working.

A society of educated, competent citizens with full access to healthcare is better for everyone, even if the newly educated and competent end up with a little attitude. Because let's face it, what we have now is a society filled with desperate, unhappy people lacking the education or healthcare they need, and there's still more than enough attitude to go around.

We may never be able to guarantee our citizens a good moral character. Let's leave that up to religion and other organizations. What the state *can* do, and must, is make sure we all have the education and medical care to succeed in life, and that we have at least the remote chance of being happy about it when we do.

The LDS Church Should Create Solar and Wind Farms

(published in the *Salt Lake Tribune* on 21 March 2020)

If there's one thing the LDS Church is good at, it's acquiring real estate. Critics find this near obsession less than Christlike, but Church leaders can transform what's currently an unflattering perception into both a financial *and* PR win. The Church can convert some of its agricultural farms and cattle ranches to solar and wind farms to lessen the impact of the climate crisis. By doing so, the Church will also create more outdoor jobs, a necessity for the foreseeable future as we adapt to the new reality of social distancing in the midst of a global pandemic.

Because the LDS Church is tight-lipped about its assets, it's difficult to know exactly how many farms and ranches it owns and operates. Different sources list 290,000 acres in one part of Florida, another 380,000 acres in another part. One source lists 200,000 acres along the Utah/Wyoming border, a tract of 288,000 acres in Nebraska, and various other farms in Canada, Argentina, Brazil, and Zimbabwe. It might be easier for Church leaders to offer transparency, an act that in itself would produce good PR, if they also revealed the contributions they're making toward generating renewable energy.

The Church could hold on to its ranches and agricultural farms suffering under changing climate conditions. Or they could sell them. But they could also convert some of them to solar and wind farms. Many farmers around the world have started combining traditional crops with solar panels, sometimes even using the panels as shade for those crops vulnerable to increasing temperatures. And there's a growing variety in types of wind turbines. The Church can continue to grow crops and raise livestock where appropriate, but it can also generate and sell power to local communities.

The Church gets money. Or it can donate energy to local communities and count that as a charitable gift.

The Church reduces the community's carbon output.

The Church creates more outdoor employment.

The Church gets positive news coverage.

The Evangelical Church in Central Germany generates all the energy its various congregations need—roughly 57 million kilowatt hours—through its own wind turbines. The oldest Presbyterian church in Cleveland, Ohio, doesn't want a turbine to mar its classic 1820 structure but does purchase its energy from a nearby wind farm. In the UK, a hundred Quaker meetinghouses have embraced renewable energy sources, as have another 900 Salvation Army buildings, over 2000 Catholic parishes, and many buildings owned by the Church of England.

The roof of a single synagogue, Temple Beth El in Stamford, Connecticut, generates over 237,000 kilowatt hours of energy a year. There are solar panel and wind turbine companies that specialize in meeting the needs of religious structures.

The LDS Church claims its multi-billion-dollar portfolios are preparation for hard times. Investing to create more outdoor jobs would help address both immediate and long-term needs in the face of the pandemic. And since even more hard times will increasingly be related to climate change, why not add investments in solar and wind power to Church portfolios? Why not add carbon capture technologies? These and other "green" enterprises are where future income lies, not fossil fuels.

The Church can also invest in geothermal power and wave energy. It can add solar panels to some of their chapels. A solitary wind turbine on every Church property could become as much of a signature as Moroni atop LDS temples. All of these actions would add to global efforts at tackling the climate crisis, making them essential *regardless* of public perception. But they'll *also* create goodwill.

Each president of the Church wants to leave a personal legacy. David O. McKay is known for bringing the 19th century Church into the 20th century. Spencer W. Kimball is known for greatly expanding the missionary program. Gordon B. Hinckley is known for his great strides in reducing societal stigma surrounding the Church.

President Nelson can be known for changing the name of the Mormon Tabernacle Choir. Or he can be known for being the tech president, for bringing the Church into the 21st century and leading the worldwide religious efforts to address our ever more desperate climate emergency, which threatens more lives and livelihoods than even the worst-case projections for the coronavirus outbreak. And that's a lot.

By their fruits ye shall know them.

Let's pray for some climate-friendly fruit.

Democratic Voters Have a New Level of Expectation

(published in *LA Progressive* on 29 March 2020)

The novel coronavirus outbreak is shining a light on what all but corporate Democrats—and truthfully, even quite a few of them—have known for some time. Unjustifiable inequality in healthcare, educational opportunity, housing, and income are damaging not only to "the poor" but to the entire country as well. As a former Republican who became a Democrat who became a Democratic Socialist, I've seen this shift to the left among a growing number of friends and acquaintances over the past decade. Some moderates still worry about progressives demanding too much from their candidates, but what was acceptable in the past is no longer sufficient. It wasn't true *before* COVID-19 cases started surging across the country, but elite Democratic leaders and corporate media can no longer prevent everyone from seeing the evidence right in front of them. Voters have a new level of expectation.

I'd already earned three English degrees before I started working on a degree in Biology. While some of my Biology Lab 1001 classmates struggled, I routinely earned a 95 or 100 on every quiz. After nine years of college classes, I knew perfectly well how to be a good student. All I had to do was review my notes three times before class and I was set.

Or so I thought.

Life changed when I enrolled in a sophomore level Cell and Molecular Physiology class. I found myself muddling along with B's until mid-term, when I finally started earning A's again. Despite all my previous coursework, much of it even at the graduate level, it turned out I still needed to up my game. Meeting with my professor in her office, I confessed, "It took a while for me to adjust to this new level of expectation."

She nodded knowingly.

In my senior level Biochemistry, I filled out almost 500 index cards per exam, drawing molecules and complicated molecular pathways. For that one class, I learned what would have equaled the coursework for three or four junior level classes.

Moderate Democrats criticize progressives for having a litmus or purity test. "It's your way or the highway," they complain. "You need to be flexible and get what you can. If you insist on all or nothing, you'll get nothing. And you'll take the rest of us down with you."

I don't know a single progressive, though, who is insisting on *everything.* Even countries with universal healthcare and tuition-free college still have plenty of problems. We're not expecting Utopia. But we do expect more than freshman or sophomore level rights.

Rights, by definition, aren't a luxury. Was there a financial cost to ending slavery? Was there a cost to gaining suffrage for women? To guaranteeing marriage equality? The specific dollar figure isn't the important question. All people deserve to be free, whether there is a small cost, a moderate cost, or any other level of cost. The truth is, when *all* costs are taken into account, it's always less expensive to "give" people basic human rights.

Too many moderates seem to have only one non-negotiable demand—that the candidate be a Democrat. When I began my Biology degree, I hadn't taken a math class since high school and needed to enroll in two remedial classes to catch up before I could tackle Physics or Chemistry. My professors didn't lower their standards. I had to rise to meet the requirements.

A remedial level of non-negotiables isn't a viable path for a Democratic candidate anymore.

But my recent conversation with a moderate gay friend didn't go well. "Would you vote for a Democrat who didn't support marriage equality?"

"We already have marriage equality."

"You didn't answer my question."

"Well, I voted for Obama before he endorsed marriage equality."

"You still haven't answered my question. Would you support a candidate *now* who spoke against same-sex marriage?"

My friend still refused to answer, so I moved on.

"Would you support a candidate who was against a woman's right to choose?"

"If my only other option was a Republican, then yes."

"And if you have other Democratic candidates who *do* support a woman's autonomy over her own body?"

My friend frowned.

"Would you vote for a Democrat who wanted to eliminate Social Security and Medicare?" I went on.

"No Democrat is going to move backward."

"Would you vote for a Democrat who refused to stop separating children from their parents? Would you vote for a Democrat who felt racial justice had already been achieved and needed no further effort? Would you vote for a Democrat who threatened to pull out of NATO? Who sold off our national parks? Who didn't believe the disabled deserved rights?"

The fact is we *all* have non-negotiables when making decisions on which candidate to support.

Healthcare is a human right. Tuition-free college and vocational training are non-negotiable. Aggressive, immediate action on the climate crisis is non-negotiable. The coronavirus shows the futility of allowing elite political leaders or corporate media to pretend these "unrealistic demands" are only items on a wish list. They are quite literally the difference between life and death, both for individuals *and* for the nation as a whole.

That's especially true for the Democratic Party, which cannot expect to pass Local or General Election 2020 if they don't meet a higher level of expectation.

My Biochemistry professor didn't grade on a curve. If we answered a complicated essay question with 95% accuracy, we didn't get any points at all for that answer. Our democracy isn't in kindergarten any longer. We're not high school students. We're not freshmen college students. We are the teachers, and we can no longer accept candidates unable to comprehend that casually reviewing their notes three times before an exam isn't going to earn them an A this time.

Voters aren't giving candidates honorary degrees. If Democratic candidates across the country want a passing grade, they must adjust to a new level of expectation.

Borrowed Emergency

(published in *LA Progressive* on 8 March 2020)

The temperature was 43 degrees in the Japanese Garden. Rain fell heavily all morning, rare for Seattle, where the precipitation most people complained about was often no more than a light drizzle. This early in the season, only a week after opening at the beginning of March, the rich, vibrant green of all the mosses on our trees and rocks and bridges was the most impressive feature of the park.

Three middle-aged women walked up to my window on their way out of the garden. "We just wanted you to know," one of the women said, "that we were very disappointed by the climate change activities today." She looked at the other two women, who nodded their agreement. "It was *very* disruptive. They were even using a *microphone*. We *came* here for the peace."

The women then walked out to their car.

This was our first Family Saturday of the year. What with the cold and the rain and the coronavirus outbreak, only a few dozen people had shown up, probably the most peaceful Saturday I'd worked at the Garden in three years. The climate change program consisted of a gentle musical performance, a bit of theater, and a few readings. The place was hardly a mosh pit.

Seattle's Japanese Garden lies beside Lake Washington Boulevard, the only thoroughfare through the Arboretum and the fastest route through this part of the city. The street is always busy during operating hours, any day of the week. The most frequent complaint we heard from visitors was about all the traffic, which produced far more noise than anything a handful of artists performing under umbrellas beside bare cherry trees could generate.

Japanese gardens typically take advantage of something called a "borrowed view." The area surrounding a garden may not officially be part of that garden, but because it can be seen from the various pathways, it becomes part of the experience. Seattle's garden, inside the 230-acre Arboretum, is surrounded by tall, lush trees and steep hills on both sides. Bald eagles and osprey sometimes fly overhead. On a good day, a blue heron might swoop down to wade in the koi pond, stalking the fish for hours. At closing time, we might see a family of raccoons making their way to the water's edge for dinner.

One famous garden in Japan is situated right next to a hospital. Part of its borrowed ambiance is the wail of emergency sirens.

The three unhappy middle-aged visitors on Family Saturday seemed to be telling me, "We *wanted* to enjoy *this* Japanese garden that's completely unaffected by climate change."

But our garden, like every other, has a "borrowed emergency," a climate crisis far more dire than the blossoming pandemic of COVID-19, as bad as that may turn out to be. During my lunch break, I caught up on the news, learning that hundreds of empty planes flew "ghost flights" over Europe because of rules which took flight slots away from airlines if their planes stayed on the ground.

My job with the Parks department requires me to walk through the entire Japanese Garden every morning before opening the gates. On a cloudy day, when I look down into the koi pond from the Moon Viewing platform, I feel I'm staring off a cliff into a bank of clouds far below. I listen to the waterfall flowing past the teahouse. I look up, beyond the borders of the garden into the Arboretum, where there are old-growth cedar, fir trees, even a few giant Sequoia.

But if you come to Seattle and stop by the Japanese Garden, don't expect it to be a refuge from the world. Even the most tranquil, apolitical spots anywhere on the face of the Earth are surrounded by climate disaster. If we want peace, and I think most of us do, we'll need to do more than complain about climate activists. We'll have to address the climate crisis itself. And it's just possible that might require us to listen to people using a microphone when reading climate poetry in the rain.

Just for the Outer Darkness of It

"Greater love hath no man than this, that a man lay down his life for a friend" (John 15:13).

A few years back, a television commercial featured a young girl watching her mother rinse the dishes before placing them in the dishwasher. "I thought the dishwasher did the dishes," the young girl says, puzzled.

"It does," the mother replies with a big smile, washing another plate before setting it in the dishwasher.

The young girl looks on in confusion.

Mormon theology explaining why we face Earthly trials is every bit as confusing.

We are deeply moved when we see stories of people sacrificing their freedom or their life for others, Corrie ten Boom hiding Jews and ultimately being sent to a concentration camp along with them, Aleksandr Solzhenitsyn sentenced to eight years of hard labor in a gulag for opposing Stalin, firefighters dying in the World Trade Center as they tried to rescue office workers. When soldiers die in battle, we commemorate them for making the ultimate sacrifice.

Mormons seem to follow this same basic line of reasoning. We think of those killed at Haun's Mill as martyrs. When one of my fellow missionaries in Italy was hit on his bicycle and killed, the rest of us were in awe that he'd died serving the

Lord. Surely, whatever sins the young man had committed, he was now assured the Celestial Kingdom.

As the years passed, though, I began questioning the suffering we all face in life, which seems far too great to serve a useful purpose. If pain and misery are supposed to be a refiner's fire, why do so many people come out of that kiln unrefined? If suffering is supposed to be the most effective teaching tool God can possibly provide, and only a small fraction of us are ever able to improve as a result, I can't help wondering if Mr. You Can Be Perfect Just Like Me! Did poorly in Celestial School.

What do you call someone who graduates last in Godhood class?

A god!

The Book of Mormon tells us that after Christ visited the Americas, the Nephites and Lamanites lived together peacefully for 200 years. They had all things in common, there was no strife, everyone was happy. So does that mean that for 200 years, no one learned a single important lesson? No one suffered enough to qualify for the Celestial Kingdom? All that peace and happiness was for nothing?

If the only way God can teach us the lessons we need is to allow other people to rob, beat, rape, torture, oppress, and kill us, he's either a terribly shitty God *or* those of us trying to be "good" are getting in his way. If people *need* to be robbed, beaten, raped, tortured, oppressed, and killed, treating them kindly is making it *harder* for them to improve their souls.

So which is it to be? God, out of the goodness of his heart, needs humans to commit barbarous atrocities *or* God, out of the shittiness of his heart, doesn't give a damn about our suffering here on Earth one shiblum.

It's a false either/or, I suppose. Another alternative is simply that God doesn't exist and therefore can't care one way or the other, that it's up to us to create a just and merciful society.

How do believing Mormons rationalize the teaching that only the kindest, most loving people make it to the Celestial Kingdom when that behavior essentially means they're only looking out for themselves? Why do we believe that the worst humans, especially apostates who break our hearts, are those who will be cast into Outer Darkness when they're the ones giving their all (their eternal happiness) to help others learn and grow?

As the non-Christian King of Siam pointed out so effectively, "It's a puzzlement."

Even more puzzling is how often I've heard from believing Mormons, even bishops, "If I stopped believing in God, there would be nothing to keep me from stealing and killing."

An odd belief, since atheists don't seem to kill in substantially different numbers than Christians. But even stranger is to recognize their lack of comprehension in the rules God set up. If that bishop did stop believing in God, and did start stealing and killing, he'd only then be helping his fellow embryonic deities return to God's presence.

And yet, with every improvement in character those larval gods make because of the ex-bishop's cruelty, they themselves then drift further from the ability to offer their own ultimate sacrifice. The nicer and more loving they become, the less they commit the atrocities that so benefit their fellow man.

It's not a vicious circle. It's a vicious-loving-vicious-loving cycle.

And *that's* the best God can come up with?

We're taught that in the pre-existence God asked for suggestions on how to help his children. One child said he'd go down and atone for their sins. Another said he'd go down and make everyone be good.

Apparently, no one else offered any suggestions. Too bad, since when we brainstorm, it's rarely the first idea that's the best.

And I have to wonder why God is asking his kids what to do in the first place. They haven't even started their Godhood coursework yet. This is *before* the War in Heaven, after all.

But I have to be grateful for these teachings, I suppose. If they weren't so maddeningly illogical, I wouldn't have been able to grow as much as I have and become the thorn in the side of my former Mormon friends who feel too much pain to associate with me any longer. Thus blessing their lives.

Just for the Outer Darkness of it, though, I wish the next prophet would start teaching something more worthwhile. Maybe about how to eradicate abuse and cruelty altogether. Because if he can't do that, he serves no useful function at all.

And that is *not* a blessing to anyone.

My HIV Infection Taught Me to Treat Everyone as if They're Contagious

(published in *LA Progressive* on 26 March 2020)

As I self-isolate at home, I see folks a block down from me hosting birthday parties. I see friends of mine getting together for various other reasons, some trying to keep a safe physical distance but others in the same group offering comforting back rubs during this stressful period. These folks want to show that they aren't afraid of their friends. They don't want to insult family members. But acting sensibly doesn't mean panicking and accusing everyone of trying to kill you. As a gay man who came out in the 1980s, I understand that the only reasonable course of action at a time like this is to assume *everyone* is infected.

By the time I came out, the AIDS pandemic was well underway. I first learned of the disease from a one-paragraph article on the back page of my hometown newspaper in late 1982. I understood the impact immediately and wondered why that information wasn't on the front page. But I knew the answer, even as a virginal, former Mormon missionary: the disease was affecting people who didn't matter, and bigotry was preventing the populace as a whole from realizing they weren't immune.

COVID-19 has become politicized as well. Perhaps it happens with every major disease. In the Middle Ages, bubonic plague was often blamed on the Jews. Hundreds of years later,

Germans blamed the French for syphilis. In 19th-century America, the Irish were blamed for cholera outbreaks. The blaming only hurt communities. It never helped.

I didn't start dating men until 1987, so I *never* had unsafe sex. It was clear that the only sensible way to interact sexually with other men was to assume they were all HIV+. Perhaps they hadn't been tested and didn't know their status. Perhaps they'd been infected since their last test. Perhaps they were lying, afraid no one would have sex with them if they told the truth. It didn't really matter. The bottom line was that the only reasonable course of action was to assume *everyone* had the virus and behave accordingly.

I admit, I had a lot of sex. Some of the other guys were negative, but a good many of them were positive. I wasn't afraid of men with HIV. I simply took precautions. There was no need to make anyone an outcast.

Even one of my long-term partners had HIV, but I never caught the virus from him. We simply made efforts to be careful.

After we broke up, though, and I was playing with others again, I made a single mistake. One. *One* mistake. Playing with two elderly neighbors, I was surprised when one of the men penetrated me without first putting on a condom.

That wasn't cool, I thought. But I didn't want to offend the guy. So I didn't insist he back out. At least for the next ten seconds. Then I repositioned myself so that my desired goal was achieved without having to say anything. That way, I didn't have to take part in an awkward conversation that might hurt his feelings.

But ten seconds was all it took. Just one encounter with an infected man during which I behaved in a foolish manner radically changed the rest of my life.

Several days later, I became ill and passed out while waiting for the health clinic to open. Even so, I thought all I had was strep throat. I'd already forgotten about those ten foolhardy seconds. So a couple of months later, when a local hospital began accepting applicants for an HIV vaccine trial, I went in to be tested. I assumed I'd still be negative, as I had been after every other test, and would therefore qualify.

I didn't qualify.

While some of my Mormon relatives believed I contracted HIV because I was a terrible sinner, the truth is I was infected because I was careless.

We can't be foolish and worry about offending our friends and family by assuming they are infected with the coronavirus. It doesn't mean we're accusing them of anything. It's not a slap in the face. It doesn't mean we think they're morally deficient in any way.

The corollary is for *us* not to feel offended when our friends and loved ones assume *we're* infected and act accordingly.

My husband and I have been together over 12 years. We only have safe sex. I am not offended because we take precautions. I'm happy that he is still HIV negative.

Many of us are going to develop COVID-19. It's far more communicable than HIV. But we can flatten the curve and make survival possible for more patients and healthcare workers if we just accept the new normal. *Immediately.*

We don't need to panic. We just need to be careful around everyone, including—no, especially—the ones we love.

Progressives Must Accept It's OK to be Hated

(published in *LA Progressive* on 25 April 2020)

Progressives give in again and again because they don't want to hold up aid, they don't want to prevent at least some token effort at solving a problem, they don't want people to think they're mean and selfish. They definitely don't want to be hated. But this constant fear makes them powerless. You can never be the alpha if you're always lying on your back exposing your stomach to show submission. Progressives need to accept that if they hope to accomplish anything meaningful, they must be willing to be hated.

"But we're the good guys!" I hear progressives say. "We're trying to make the world a better place! How can we do that if people hate us?"

First of all, we need to accept the reality that people *already* hate us. Those on the right do, without a doubt. But a great many moderate Democrats do as well. Don't you hear it in the disdain with which they dismiss our reluctance to support Biden as the Democratic nominee? "You say there's not much difference between Republicans and Democrats? Well, I say there's not much difference between a progressive who won't vote for Biden and an idiot who votes for Trump." I was told that by one of my longtime "friends." She has no trouble being hated, takes it as a badge of honor.

While I wonder about her strategy of bringing progressives to her side by calling them idiots, I do think she's onto something by not being "nice" all the time. Krystal Ball, on her show "Rising," finally helped me understand the power we can wield if we are willing to be hated. If we cede all our power by placating bullies, either those on the right or those in the middle, we end up pleasing no one. The right still hates us. The corporate centrists see us as their "bitches," and progressives are disappointed we've failed them yet again.

Most of us on the far left *are* nice people. When we make people mad, when we upset them, we are usually humble enough to question our behavior. Are we in fact doing something wrong? We don't want to be bullies ourselves. But this constant second-guessing and waffling robs us of the power to accomplish anything meaningful. Those times we *are* wrong, we need to adjust our ideas. But that shouldn't be 99% of the time.

I was the only Mormon in my Baptist High School. As a senior, I came in second place for Most Popular. Frankly, I was surprised even to do that well. I was more disappointed to come in second for Best Christian Example. I really wanted to be first in that.

I did, though, end up as Most Courteous on the senior superlatives page of our yearbook.

Sally Field's Oscar acceptance speech—"You *like* me! You really, really like me!"—resonated with the audience because we understand how desperately everyone wants to be liked.

But did the Tea Party worry about being liked or did they worry about getting legislation passed that they wanted? Do

Republicans worry about not offending Democrats? Does Trump worry about looking "mean"?

We certainly don't need to be cruel just for the sake of cruelty. We don't need to be cruel at all. But we do need to stand firm on what is right, *even if* other political leaders on "our" side hate us for it.

Even if we alienate a family member or lose a friend.

As a Mormon, I was always taught that family was the highest good in life. David O. McKay, one of our prophets, claimed that "No other success can compensate for failure in the home."

Several of my closest family members haven't spoken to me in years because I won't back down on gay rights. That was painful. But I got the fuck over it and moved on.

We must be willing to be abandoned even by the people we love *if* we expect to champion the rights of the poor, the sick, the oppressed, and anyone else crushed by right-wing Republicans *and* corporate Democrats.

Every day on the news, I watch anchors and pundits wail about how awful Trump is. They always ask some form of the question, "Can we finally now agree that Trump is bad?" Hey, guys, you proved that *three years ago* and *every day* since then. Can we *please* shift the conversation to solutions?

And stop telling me the solution is to give in to moderate Democrats who don't get us what we need. "Trump won't get it for us, so you have to vote for us!" But they won't get it for us, either. How do we know? Because we see the evidence every day. Moderate candidates won't even put Medicare for All on their platform. Or tuition-free college. Or a Green New Deal.

To be nice to their corporate donors. They certainly aren't being nice to their prospective constituents.

And those already in office aren't failing to pass good pandemic aid packages because more people on the other side are voting against their wishes. *They're* voting against anything good in those bills, too.

To be nice. To placate. To not look like bullies. To not be the bad guys holding up aid.

And the result?

They hold up aid and any meaningful legislation to improve our lives.

I imagine my moderate political friends singing the Mormon hymn, "There is beauty all around when there's love at home."

With love like this, who needs hate?

Just like my Mormon family, moderate Democrats tell us every day, "If you just repent and come back into the fold, we'll like you again."

Yeah, don't do me any favors.

You want my financial contribution to your campaign? You want my vote? You want my power? Then don't tell me to roll over and offer you my throat. Give me something worth my money, my vote, my power.

Because if you don't, you've proven you already hate me anyway.

Which Scrooge Are You?

(published in *LA Progressive* on 4 April 2020)

At the beginning of Charles Dickens's *A Christmas Carol*, when Ebenezer Scrooge contemplates the death of his employee's ill child and many others like him, he says dismissively, "If they would rather die, they had better do it, and decrease the surplus population." Scrooge, of course, is concerned only about making money, whatever the consequences to others. He begrudges Bob Cratchit enough coal to heat his office. He complains about giving his clerk a day off to celebrate the birth of Jesus with his family. He suggests that the poor might be better off in prison.

Here at the start of the COVID-19 pandemic, we're already hearing corporate and political leaders insisting we open businesses again as soon as possible, often weeks or even months before health officials deem it safe. Some governors don't even want to close down in the first place. "The cure" will be worse than the pandemic, they claim. Think of the people who will die because they've lost their jobs, become homeless, become depressed and suicidal over their financial circumstances. Business leaders whose actions never took into account the sufferings of the poor before insist they are now doing folks a *favor* by forcing them back to work. Several prominent older folks with plenty of insurance and money to stay holed up for months nobly and publicly pretend they're willing to give up their own lives "for the country."

Of course, gold promoters like Glenn Beck and conservative politicians like Dan Patrick won't be the ones dying. It will be the poor or nearly poor who have no choice but to risk infection every day at work who will do most of the dying.

Along with a good many middle-class folks who adhere to various iterations of the prosperity gospel, afraid that a temporary reduction in funds will indicate a loss of favor with their God.

Voluntary as well as conscripted risk takers all working together to decrease the surplus population.

The White House has no problem throwing trillions of dollars at Wall Street for the good of the country. But suspending (not postponing) rent payments for residents? And lease payments for small businesses? Absolving student loan debt? Tying the trillions bestowed upon corporations to mandatory paychecks for employees? The only reason anyone would lose their job, become homeless, or become depressed or suicidal over their financial situation is if we insist on making sure their financial situation remains dire.

That's a choice, not a natural consequence of pandemics. Other countries, like Denmark and Belgium and the Netherlands, have made a different choice, one that prioritizes people over profits. Or at least puts them *somewhere* on the list of priorities.

At some point, people will obviously need to go back to work. Society can't function indefinitely without labor. But a few weeks into a war against a deadly pathogen is hardly the time for capitulation. Friends of mine, even some colleagues from my Mormon missionary days, talk about the need to sacrifice those most vulnerable for the sake of "the country."

Those with chronic health problems are unhappy in the best of times. The elderly have already had their chance at life. They'll only be around a few more years anyway. Why should the rest of us suffer because grandma wants to play with her grandchildren? She can see them just fine from heaven.

While people of any age can become seriously ill or die from COVID-19, the death rate starts rising sharply for people 60 and over. I realize many Americans lack proficiency in math, but do we need a scientist to point out that a 60-year-old could easily live another 30 years? The "elderly" are not at death's door and simply being pushed through a few days early. Even a 70-year-old with diabetes could have several good years left. Mary Tyler Moore lived to be 80. Do we really want to tell folks like Laura Petrie and Mary Richards, "We liked you in your prime, but we have no further use for you, so goodbye and good luck"?

My conservative and religious friends often claim that all abortion is murder. *They* value the sanctity of life. Apparently, though, life loses its divine stamp of approval if it interferes with corporate profits. Children get little societal assistance once they're out of the womb. Even in the midst of massive layoffs, with people around the world dying from the coronavirus by the thousands, my conservative family can't accept that tying health insurance to the workplace is a fundamentally flawed policy.

Fortunately, health officials have insisted that we not send people back to non-essential jobs to infect each other just yet. So for now, we can still sit at home and read a good book. Maybe something inspirational from Dickens. Ebenezer Scrooge did, after all, learn to value life in the end. And an early novel by the author of *Robinson Crusoe*, who clearly understood something about social distancing, might be enlightening as well. Perhaps his *Journal of the Plague Year*.

If we want to do something as a family, though, something *fun*, we can always watch a comedy together. *Throw Momma from the Train* is trending heavily right now.

Who Said It Best—Republicans or Democrats?

(published in *LA Progressive* on 6 May 2020)

"All Lives Matter!"

"My Body, My Choice!"

"Believe Women!"

In one episode of the popular television series, *The Big Bang Theory*, Howard teases Raj by asking the gang to guess whom he was addressing when he made various comments—his beloved dog or his beautiful girlfriend. "Emily or Cinnamon?" Howard asks. "'How could such a little girl eat such a big steak?'" The humor stretches throughout the episode as again and again, the gang has trouble deciding who was the intended recipient.

Similarly, as Americans struggle through the pandemic, we hear protesters and activists every day on the news and have a surprisingly difficult time figuring out who made a particular declaration. "All Lives Matter!" Oh, that's the platitude from the right, we remember, when certain white folks try to deny the bias that leads to unprovoked killings of people of color.

But no, this time it was said by someone on the left, urging conservatives not to "restart" the economy too soon, to reconsider their willingness to sacrifice additional tens of thousands of lives—lives of the elderly, diabetics, those with asthma, lives of poor people, ethnic minorities, asylum seekers, and inmates. Lives of medical professionals.

When Republican leaders organize to discuss how many COVID-19 deaths are acceptable, could that be considered a "death panel"?

If "an injustice anywhere is a threat to justice everywhere," does being required to wear a mask in public constitute "injustice"?

We're hearing people at "Liberate our state!" rallies shouting, "My body, my choice!" It's jarring to hear, of course, as only a few months ago, these freedom fighters were enraged when women claimed the same right.

Likewise, it used to be Democrats who insisted we give sexual assault victims a fair hearing when they accuse powerful men. But now it seems they want to brush credible accusations aside when *their* guy faces scrutiny.

Democrats dismiss Fox News as partisan, but if Chris Hayes simply reports on Joe Biden's accuser, there's an immediate call to MSNBC for his dismissal. "He's not supporting Democrats!"

The list goes on, Republicans and Democrats playing "Who wore it best?" on the red carpet of punditry.

"You need to respect the office of the President!"

"We're the ones looking out for your best interests."

"It's the *way* they're protesting that's inappropriate."

Emily or Cinnamon? Like Penny, we find the questions much more difficult than they first appear.

Are those waving Confederate flags patriots or are they traitors?

Do Democrats really believe science if they won't stop supporting fossil fuel corporations?

Is it a cheap shot to call folks waving a swastika at a "reopen" rally Nazis? Is a sign at the rally proclaiming *Arbeit macht frei* truly pro-freedom or is it actually pro-genocide?

I *wish* this game was merely "Republicans or Democrats?" but it seems to have quickly devolved into something far more sinister.

The cultural divide in America has become surreal, creating a Bizarro world like that which confused Elaine Benes on *Seinfeld*. For as long as I can remember, extremists on the far right were hoarding food and guns and ammo, preparing to hunker down and shelter in place when an inevitable global crisis arrived. And yet now, so many of these same people use the weapons they've amassed to demand haircuts. They want to go to the mall. They want chicken wings.

Republicans argue that business should "return to normal" because the stress of staying closed will lead to depression and suicide. Yet they seem to have no problem with a "normal" that requires school children to cower under their desks during active shooter drills. Or, worse, flee actual shooters. But maybe that isn't such a novel position, after all. The truth is that conservative values often sacrifice the innocent.

The residents of Flint get poisoned water so those in power can save money. The poor and those who lose their jobs get no healthcare so that corporations can improve profits. Our groundwater, air, and land are polluted so that the wealthy can become wealthier. Public schools in poor neighborhoods get less money so that children from wealthier areas can maintain their advantage.

All in the name of freedom.

But with freedom like this, who needs oppression?

And oddly, the DNC takes money from all the same corrupting influences. They decry the high price of prescription drugs but only the far left "fringe" raises the idea of universal healthcare. Democrats demand "transparency" from the Trump administration and yet have no problem with Biden refusing access to the records where Tara Reade's official complaint might reside.

When Emily confronts Raj's friends after a day of relentless teasing, she says she loves that her boyfriend is so sweet to both her and the dog. She kisses the likable loser full on the lips in front of his friends as a reward.

And then backs away, her nose wrinkled in disgust as she pulls something off her tongue. "Why do you have dog hair in your mouth?"

Perhaps the problem with understanding the real values of either Republicans or Democrats is that their slogans only serve the underlying function of emotionally appeasing the masses while still directing every resource that matters to those in power.

The game isn't nearly as funny in real life.

We Can't *Eliminate* Our Impact on Climate, but We *Can* Lessen It

(published in *LA Progressive* on 3 May 2020)

Some climate activists grow discouraged when they discover that wind, solar, wave, and thermal energy technologies each carry their own damaging limitations. But that's no reason to give up on renewables. The only way to completely eliminate the negative consequences of human activity on the planet...is to eliminate humans. Short of that, the best we can do is reduce the damage. A transition away from fossil fuels is an essential step forward.

Harm reduction is a term describing the effort to help those addicted to drugs without expecting to solve the problem. For instance, while it's better if a person stops shooting up altogether, if that's not feasible simply by hoping or praying—or punishing—then the next best thing is to make shooting up less destructive. We provide clean needles and a "safe" place to inject, perhaps have someone nearby ready with naloxone. It's not ideal, but if we can reduce some of the worst consequences of addiction, we have a better chance at reaching the most vulnerable and eventually finding better solutions.

Michael Moore's film *Planet of the Humans* suggests technology isn't an answer to the climate crisis. We must instead significantly decrease the global population and live in harmony with nature. Is the solution then to bioengineer a more powerful disease than COVID-19? Carbon emissions had begun rising significantly even by the year 1900, when there were fewer than two billion people on the planet. It might be difficult to rally people behind killing four or five billion of their fellow man. Even if all 7.7 billion of us here today gave up technology, we'd *still* create havoc with the environment. It would be a different type of damage, and maybe a lesser one in regard to carbon, but we'd still leave our mark, and it wouldn't be pretty.

Remember how the fields at Woodstock looked in 1969?

All other things being equal, what's better for a forest? Cutting down twenty-four trees or three hundred and sixty-two?

What's a better outcome for a nuclear war? Three destroyed cities or seven hundred?

Would you rather your hometown suffer a 5.1 magnitude earthquake or an 8.4?

A simplified example of chaos theory is the butterfly flapping its wings in China and then through a series of unpredictable cause and effect repercussions, it rains in France. The truth is we're *going* to have a negative impact on the environment and climate. We *can*, though, mitigate the damage. That mitigation will inevitably cause unexpected damage, and we'll need to find a way to lessen that. Then *that* mitigation will need tweaking as well. But we don't give up making improvements just because the next step forward isn't 100% perfect.

Perhaps we can't stop the impact of all fossil fuel extraction already in process, but we can certainly refuse to add to the problem. When our frying pan catches fire while we're cooking dinner, we don't pour a bottle of vegetable oil on it to douse the flames. We don't pour water, either. But there *are* options to limit the damage.

We must immediately stop making the worst climate choices possible—oil, coal, fracking, even nuclear with its radioactive waste and potential for sabotage.

Do we refuse to support renewable energy technology because it's developed and sold by corporations? Waiting until the U.S. and other capitalist countries convert to socialism before we begin a full-fledged transition away from fossil fuels is suicide. Yes, it may take such a conversion to repair the worst damage, but we can't wait until conditions are perfect before we take action.

We certainly can't wait a hundred years for a global one-child policy to reduce the human population to a healthier level, as essential as that may be in an overall plan.

Our best options at the moment for reducing the catastrophic impact of our presence on the planet are wind, solar, wave, and thermal energy technologies. But even if we completely convert the entire globe to these renewables in the next ten years, that will hardly be the end of human progress. Technology didn't stop with the invention of the wheel or the discovery of fire. It didn't end with pulleys or levers or the steam engine. And it won't stop when we transition away from fossil fuels.

This adaptation *cannot possibly* be perfect. Neither will the next one or the one after that.

None of that means it's okay to construct a single new pipeline or drill even one more well.

We can't eliminate greed or stupidity, either, but we'd sure better find a way to lessen their destructive impact.

Or perhaps we *will* choose a massive human death toll, after all. By default.

Harm reduction works for people and it works for climate, too. So let's develop the renewables we can and start reducing harm before we overdose on the status quo.

Lotteries Are Essential…but They Shouldn't Be

(published in *LA Progressive* on 22 April 2020)

State and national lotteries are still open during the pandemic, considered essential businesses. And they *are* essential. The problem is they *shouldn't* be. The lottery website asks players not to make a special trip just to purchase a ticket, to buy tickets only when they are part of a planned visit to the grocery store or gas station. But that's rather like a television ad for alcohol showing people partying to excess and concluding with, "Please drink responsibly."

We all know that human psychology is complex, that people still smoke despite the Surgeon General's warning on every package of cigarettes, despite commercials showing throat cancer survivors puffing out of a hole carved into their neck.

I've been at church gatherings where someone will offer a benediction over the refreshment table. "Heavenly Father, we ask thee to bless this food that it will strengthen and nourish our bodies." Then everyone digs into the potato chips and doughnuts.

Lotteries take advantage of our deeply ingrained ability to ignore the truth. So do politicians.

I continue to buy lottery tickets during the pandemic, even knowing I'm risking my health and the health of my husband. Why do I behave so irresponsibly? Why am I so cavalier about the danger to myself and others?

I do it because I'm desperate.

Even before the pandemic, I was barely getting by with two part-time jobs paying only slightly above minimum wage. At the age of 59, I'm still paying down my student loan. I have no siding on one wall of my house. I'm on public transportation. I've lost one of my jobs to the virus and may lose the other. I'm still eight years away from Social Security, assuming the program hasn't been completely gutted by then.

So I walk twenty-five minutes to the closest grocery to buy lottery tickets and another twenty-five minutes back.

Even as I acknowledge my difficult circumstances, I think of the undocumented workers who can't get any assistance at all. I think of asylum-seekers trapped in conditions that will kill a third of them once the virus starts sweeping through detention centers. I think of the millions of prisoners with convictions for non-violent offenses who are sitting ducks in confinement. I think about how those released early have nowhere to go. I think of all the other homeless folks in the U.S.

Most of the people demanding we "reopen the economy" don't have a death wish. Some, of course, are deluded by the false information they receive from right-wing corporate media. But others simply realize the government isn't going to help them. Their anger, however, is misplaced. What they should be demanding is universal healthcare, fair wages, a universal basic income, dismissal of student loans, and higher taxes on the rich. When we see 22 million new unemployment claims simultaneously with a steep rise in the stock market, we know that a "successful economy" does not include us.

I'm not the only person buying lottery tickets, but we try to stay six feet apart in line.

My sister, an LPN at a nursing home, is out with a suspected case of COVID-19. Suspected, not confirmed, because of the difficulty in obtaining a test. She gets no health insurance from her employer, hasn't seen a doctor in *years*. Even the ACA hasn't been any help, as she's never been able to afford the policies offered. It was cheaper for her to pay the tax penalty and *not* get coverage for her money.

In the movie *Logan's Run*, almost every citizen is killed when they reach the age of thirty. A few people, though, have a fighting chance, if they participate in a game that has them flying up through the air trying to reach the lone prize. As spectators watch, the contestants are zapped to death, one by one. During the course of the film, the hero discovers to his dismay that *no one* ever wins.

The regional lottery office one town over from me is closed until the pandemic is over. If I do somehow end up with a winning ticket, I'll need to take public transportation to the state capitol to claim it.

In 1991, when Klansman David Duke ran for governor of Louisiana, former governor Edwin Edwards, known for his corruption, saw a chance at re-election. One of the unofficial slogans of the campaign was, "Vote for the crook. It's important."

Edwards, who loved his trips to Las Vegas, never wasted a single dollar on the lottery. He understood gambling well enough to realize what the odds of winning actually were.

One of the courses that drove up my student loan balance was Statistics. I understand the odds, too.

But there is another lottery tonight, and I've already bought a ticket.

Maybe *this* time, I'll win. My money troubles will be over, and I'll finally be free to retire immediately.

To spend my remaining years a witness to the horrors caused by an economic and political system that feasts on the misery of the poor.

Unless we become as relentless in changing the world as a novel coronavirus.

Republicans Need to Take Responsibility for Their Actions…and So Do Democrats

(published in *LA Progressive* on 12 April 2020)

Democrats were up in arms over Republicans forcing voters to the polls in Wisconsin during a pandemic. And they were right. What the Republicans did was an outrage. The GOP needs to take responsibility for this atrocity and the many others they commit that destroy lives and livelihoods every day.

But Democrats need to stop blaming Republicans for their own multitude of failures. It's not the GOP's fault that Democrats don't push for fare-free public transit. It's not the GOP's fault that Democrats don't ban fracking. It's not the GOP's fault that Democrats don't demand ranked choice voting.

As a gay man excommunicated by the Mormon Church for coming out, I heard friends and family testify that AIDS was the natural result of sin. Sure, gay men were free to sin if we chose, but we weren't free to escape the consequences of our actions. *We* were responsible for everything bad in our lives.

So I watch in amazement as conservative religious leaders insist on gathering large congregations in the midst of a pandemic. They have freedom of religion, they insist defiantly. Atheists are just trying to persecute them by banning large groups. "Christians aren't afraid of dying," we hear them say.

Most Christian religions, though, frown on suicide. Gambling, too. I would think Russian roulette falls under at least one of those proscriptions.

If aborting a fetus is a mortal sin, isn't it also immoral to behave in a manner known to spread a deadly pathogen? Sure, Pastor Bill didn't put a gun to Grandma's head and pull the trigger, but wouldn't it still be a sin to pour cyanide into a community's water supply, even if he didn't target Grandma specifically?

The Las Vegas shooter wasn't aiming at a specific person. He just sprayed death randomly into the crowd, killing 58 people and injuring hundreds more.

When parents complain about the quality of schools in poor neighborhoods, conservatives accuse them of blaming others for their own circumstances. Poor folks are poor, conservatives say, because they have a bad work ethic, because they don't apply themselves in school, because they waste their money on cell phones. "Society" isn't responsible for the poor, they insist. Conservatives certainly aren't responsible. Poor people have no one to blame but themselves. They need to take responsibility.

And yet conservatives have no problem when President Trump refuses to accept responsibility for any of his administration's failures regarding the pandemic. First, he says the coronavirus isn't a problem. It's being overstated by Democrats who want to attack him. Then he says it *is* a problem, and he's said so all along. Then he says China lied and didn't tell him how serious the problem was. Then he says the problem isn't so bad and he wants to open up businesses and churches by Easter. Then he says we're facing one of the worst crises in our country's history. Then he says the lack of testing and masks and ventilators is the CDC's fault, Obama's fault, the fault of governors, the fault of medical personnel. Then he says he's made sure hospitals have what they need. Then he blames the WHO for not alerting him in time to prevent the virus from becoming a problem in the U.S.

It's always someone else's fault. Conservatives don't believe in taking responsibility for their actions.

They *do* believe, however, that *poor* people are responsible for *their* problems. They believe gay people are responsible. Women impregnated by rapists are responsible. Refugees fleeing violence in their countries of origin are responsible. Students racking up forty thousand dollars in debt are responsible. People who lose their health insurance when their jobs are terminated are responsible.

Corporations, of course, are *not* responsible. Banks aren't responsible. The wealthy aren't responsible.

The Democratic National Committee blames Bernie supporters for Hillary Clinton's loss in 2016. They blame Comey. They blame Putin. They blame the Electoral College. They blame young people who didn't vote. They refuse to accept responsibility for barring Sanders supporters during the primary. Worse, they refuse to accept responsibility for nominating a candidate who wasn't offering what voters wanted. That might not have been Sanders, but it certainly wasn't Clinton.

The DNC's presumptive nominee in 2020 is Joe Biden. If he doesn't win the general election, the DNC will blame Bernie supporters again. They'll blame Russia. They'll blame the Electoral College. They'll blame COVID-19.

Whatever the reason, it *won't* be because they chose to push a lackluster candidate without the vision necessary to solve problems like equal access to healthcare and education. It won't be because they chose not to address systemic racism or tackle the climate crisis head on.

People in recovery learn that they must stop blaming others for the problems in their lives. They must accept their part in those failures. They understand that making amends is part of recovery. And they know they can rely on one another to get through the hard times.

Democrats have no control over what Republicans do or don't do. They only have control over their own choices. If they want to regain power to shape society, they must stop blaming others for their inadequate platform and instead offer the people of this country what they need.

I Hope They Call Me on a Thermal Mission

(published in the *Salt Lake Tribune* on 24 April 2020)

As I watched entire planeloads of Mormon missionaries returning early, I wondered aloud to my RM husband, "How is Church culture going to handle losing this rite of passage?" Record numbers of young men have already been returning home early these past few years, more and more choosing not to serve a mission at all. Anecdotal evidence (the only evidence available given the Church's secrecy) suggests members in general have been leaving the Church "in droves."

But perhaps there's a way the Church can survive both the coronavirus and the abundance of information easily accessible via the internet.

The LDS Church has a long history of accomplishing incredible feats, from the settling of the intermountain west to photographing genealogical records across the world to sending out tens of thousands of volunteer missionaries every year. During the COVID-19 pandemic, the Mormon Church can use its organizational skills and devoted membership to help society transition away from fossil fuels by calling young men and women to serve as "renewable energy missionaries."

We've already shown we can make tremendous changes almost overnight. No more General Conference gatherings, no more weekly church meetings, no more early morning Seminary, no more temple work.

But committed members of the Church still want to serve, and Church leaders can channel that energy and dedication in other positive directions. Since the climate crisis threatens more death and destruction than even worst-case scenarios for the coronavirus, we have no choice but to transition toward renewables. And since the Church cannot send missionaries on proselyting missions anytime soon, the Church, the members, and the world can all benefit from calling members to transform Church ranches and agricultural farms into wind, solar, and even thermal energy farms.

In the long history of Mormon missionary work, we've adapted many times already. We've sent men into the world "without purse or scrip," sent men on three-year missions, sent missionaries out with no language training, sent women out as well, changed the age for missionary service, sent out married couples, sent missionaries to construct chapels, sent out "health" missionaries, sent missionaries out to do a wide variety of tasks apart from proselyting.

For the foreseeable future, we'll need more outdoor employment. The Church can acquire thousands of hours of labor from volunteers to help defray the cost of the necessary energy conversion. This type of missionary work will also teach young people job skills they'll need after the global depression we are likely to experience. Calling members on renewable energy missions is a victory on every level.

Older folks who wish to serve, or younger folks with physical limitations, can still do so by handling supply orders or monitoring information or performing other functions that don't require heavier physical labor.

And some missionaries, of course, can still serve online missions. Perhaps even these renewable energy missionaries can spend one day a week proselyting online. Others can sharpen their persuasive skills and then petition state and federal governments to do their part in helping society transition to renewables. Proselyting missionaries are essentially lobbyists anyway. The Missionary Training Center's teaching program won't require much adaptation at all—other than a shift to more online learning. There is much work to be done by a volunteer missionary workforce, all of which benefits the Church and its members both now and in the future.

I served two years as a missionary forty years ago. It remains one of the most profound experiences of my life more than three decades after I left the Church. I belong to a Facebook group for those who served under my mission president, and I'm astounded that several of the young men and women I didn't expect to remain active more than a few months after they returned home are *still* devout members all these years later.

Missionary work can bring converts to the Church, but that's not its only function. It also helps young men and women take an active, meaningful part in a noble endeavor. They work hard, they sacrifice, and they are permanently changed by the process. If Church leaders want their young people to stay committed to the organization, they need to begin offering something genuinely useful that can counterbalance the secularization of society and the unrelenting availability of unexpurgated Church history online.

Door to door, in-person missionary work will not be feasible for quite some time and might be doomed even apart from the current pandemic. But the Church can still serve its members and the rest of the world by channeling the devotion and goodwill of its missionaries into helping society transition to renewables, an evolution we *must* make in the next few years regardless.

Mormons pride themselves on being the same in every congregation around the world. We teach the same lessons, sing the same hymns, read the same scriptures, believe the same doctrine. But Mormons also have two centuries of major adaptation. Moving from New York to Pennsylvania to Ohio to Missouri to Illinois to Utah, transitioning from monogamy to polygamy to monogamy, even transitioning from hiding the history of the First Vision to becoming more transparent.

We can do this.

Let's start calling members to serve renewable energy missions.

Stop Being Defensive—Privilege Doesn't Mean Life is Perfect

Many whites become defensive when they hear they lead privileged lives. "I'm poor! I have an eating disorder! My parents beat me! I never had a chance to go to college!"

White privilege doesn't mean life is perfect. It means skin color hasn't been one of the negative factors creating challenges at every stage of our lives.

I'm right-handed. I didn't choose to be right-handed. But I didn't understand the privilege that being right-handed afforded me until I reached college and saw a left-handed desk for the first time. It baffled me why anyone would design a desk so poorly. Even then, it didn't occur to me that left-handed people needed such a design until someone pointed it out.

Privilege is not having to think about something because it's just never been an issue. Most scissors are designed for right-handed people. Even the act of writing itself (at least in English) is designed for right-handed people. It wasn't until I noticed a left-handed person writing—in college!—her left hand moving directly over the fresh ink, smudging it, that I recognized even such a simple, basic act could be a legitimate challenge.

Conspirators didn't sit in a secret meeting planning how to make life difficult for left-handed people. "Hey! I know! We'll write from left to right!" Some difficulties people face may in fact be designed out of malice, but most just develop "naturally." Still, the lack of malevolence doesn't negate the need to address them.

When I sang in a community chorus, one of the other chorus members had perfect pitch. He couldn't understand why everyone else was unable to perform at his level.

As a Mormon missionary in Italy, I couldn't understand why some of my fellow missionaries had so much difficulty learning Italian. It was an easy language. I even did well studying Russian and Hebrew, though Hebrew was challenging because it's written right to left.

As missionaries, we could clearly see that Catholics in Italy enjoyed privilege that local LDS members didn't. The way Catholics and Jews and Muslims and others can see instantly that there is Mormon privilege in Utah.

Should we feel guilty if we have perfect pitch? Are we bad people for being right-handed? Am I a terrible person because learning languages comes easily to me?

Being privileged for any quality or talent or biological fact does not mean we've done something wrong. White people need to stop feeling defensive when someone points out our privilege. It may sound like an accusation, but it's simply a statement of fact. We *are* privileged. Our society favors us. We may never have deliberately done anything to earn the favor or to create disfavor toward others, but we do benefit from the privilege that exists.

It's OK to say so.

And it doesn't mean everything else in our life has gone beautifully. Someone with white skin can also be hearing impaired. He or she might be transgender or allergic to nuts or dyslexic or have any number of other challenges.

Some people have an eidetic memory. What kind of difficulties would many of us face if society was shaped assuming *everyone* had an eidetic memory?

Some people are able to smell things the rest of us can't. Some can smell Parkinson's disease in people years before any medical tests can diagnose it. Some can smell cancer. What would life be like if the only way to successfully navigate the world was to be able to detect diseases by smell months or years before science could diagnose them?

Just because the privilege white people in Western culture enjoy is more common and more normalized doesn't make it any less arbitrary.

The only behavior that can be considered a fault on our part is feeling so defensive that we refuse to treat others equally, whatever the color of their skin, or their ability to sing, or their religion, or their ability to walk, or anything else.

Having privilege doesn't make us bad people. And if we feel any need to prove that, then let's do so by using our privilege to change the systems and rules which perpetuate discrimination against anyone.

The Democratic Party Can't Be Changed from Within

(published in *LA Progressive* on 21 May 2020)

When leftists complain that liberal Democratic candidates aren't bold enough once in office, we're told that change takes time and is only effective if it comes from within. If these liberals are too bold, they tell us, they can't be insiders and will lose what little power they have. The problem is that they willingly give up their power to be an insider in the first place, securing their own failure from the start.

Elected Democratic leaders keep voting for pandemic relief packages that overwhelmingly benefit corporations at the expense of the people, promising that "next time" they'll insist on a better deal. This behavior, though, pre-dates the pandemic by decades. The public health crisis is just the latest excuse. Liberals and progressives had to vote for this bad deal first to earn the power to say, "*Now* you owe me a favor." But when the next package deal comes up, still overwhelmingly in favor of corporations, our Democratic saviors again vote for it, telling us once more that the "next time" will be different. Even when offering a fake proposal for the following relief bill, Democratic leaders *still* don't include the programs and policies necessary to address real needs, and *this* is in the "showy" package, the one everyone knows will need to be renegotiated before it gets passed. They simply can't be bothered to pretend they care about our priorities.

Even Lucy van Pelt was more convincing when asking Charlie Brown to kick the football.

I was excommunicated from the Mormon Church over thirty years ago for being gay, but for decades I kept writing stories about "progressive" Mormons, hoping that Mormons reading my books would slowly move to the left. Organizations like Affirmation for LGBTQ Mormons tried to work "from the inside" as well. As did Family Fellowship, the Mormon equivalent to PFLAG. Mormons Building Bridges tried a similar approach, as did Mama Dragons. All these organizations, and other writers like myself, tried to effect change "from inside." *Sunstone* magazine has been publishing since 1975, and almost no "active" Mormons have even heard of it.

The problem is that once a Mormon, or worse, an ex-Mormon, says *anything* contrary to official policy, they are automatically seen as outsiders whose words must immediately be discounted. It's *impossible* to change policies on LGBTQ issues from the inside. It's impossible to effect change even on the rights of heterosexual women from the inside. Mormon feminists have been excommunicated for such heresy.

If one day the Mormon Church makes any significant changes, they will *only* come from leaders at the top. I could hang around another thirty years in docile anticipation, but I won't live that long. So I invest my efforts to make the world a better place elsewhere. A remote chance of success is better than none.

Liberal and progressive Democrats will also have a greater chance of success once they realize the same thing applies to them.

Democratic outsiders, the rebels, the troublemakers, are squashed again and again until they are finally offered a tiny bit of power. They're appointed to this committee or that task force, *if* they promise to toe the line. So they do, because they know that this act of compromise will mean Democratic leadership now owes them a favor.

But moral clarity and the strength it provides are what become compromised. In the film version of John Grisham's *The Firm*, Tom Cruise's character is enticed by all the perks he gets from joining a prestigious law firm. He isn't ethically compromised yet, but when the senior partners begin suspecting he won't remain loyal, they set him up with a beautiful woman confiding a heartrending sob story.

The Tom Cruise character has sex with the woman, which is of course all caught on film, and now the firm has leverage against him. If he doesn't do as they say, they'll go to his wife.

When liberal Democrats we've voted for cheat on us, it's not easy to forgive. Especially if they insist on continuing an open relationship without our consent.

I don't want a candidate or elected official to *say* the right things in a speech, no matter how eloquently he or she says it. What matters is the vote. *Every single time.* On a pre-employment integrity test, what's the correct answer for the following question:

You know you could skim a little money from several large accounts without being noticed. Do you

skim the accounts every chance you get?

skim the accounts only twice a year?

skim the accounts once and never again?

enlist someone else to skim the accounts so that your hands are clean?

The answer "None of the above" never seems to be an option in the world of politics. But compromising your ethics can only weaken your ability to command from the moral high ground, never strengthen it.

Not voting for an inadequate relief package when everyday people desperately need *some* relief means you'll get some flak. But haven't any of these "rebels" noticed they're already getting flak every day? They tell us that minimal relief is better than none, so they must get *something* in the hands of the poor immediately. They promise to get us a better deal "next time."

I see Lucy van Pelt holding the football again.

Every single time you vote against the needs of the people in favor of corporations and their owners, you give opponents anywhere on the political spectrum ammunition against you. "So-and-so *says* they're for student loan forgiveness. But look how they voted on this piece of legislation."

Those who hate you, those who have never supported you, won't suddenly support you because you've been broken into submission. They'll stick with the candidates who were on their side from the start. And those who used to believe in you will have lost faith in anything you tell them. Yes, you *say* you've learned your lesson, but I won't know if that's true until *after* the next election. You burned me before. Maybe this other candidate will, too, but if I must take a chance, I'll go with the one who hasn't burned me yet.

There are those on the left who hope that if enough Democrats leave the party, its leaders will realize the error of their ways and change. Who knows? Maybe they will and maybe they won't. But it's pointless to wait. The carrot on the end of a stick never gets any closer.

In the last fifteen to twenty years, Mormons have been leaving their church in droves. And what have Church leaders who see this departure done? Well, they now allow sister missionaries to wear slacks…sometimes. Black members can now wear "black hairstyles" inside the temple. And teenage girls can now hand out towels in the temple, a privilege once denied them. That's all new. Groundbreaking. But leggings for women in their daily lives? No, that's a bridge too far. Women who commit such sin still need to confess to their bishop and repent. Beards for male BYU students? Such a violation of the Honor Code will still get them expelled from college.

I'm not wasting any more time on vain hopes for improvement from within. Not in the Mormon Church and not in the Democratic Party.

Last night, my ex-Mormon husband and I watched *Monsters University*. One throwaway scene near the beginning shows a slug "racing" to his first class. He arrives in the final minute of the film, after the semester is over and everyone else has gone home.

Despite its many flaws, I enjoyed being part of the Mormon Church and hated to leave, especially since so many people I love and respect are still believers. But my life is immeasurably better since. Liberals and progressives need to consider that leaving the Democratic Party may be a more successful path for them as well. The one thing we can be sure of, unfortunately, is that staying won't accomplish anything that's meaningful—because it isn't "time" Democratic leaders need. It's the opportunity to keep supporting their corporate donors.

Do We Really *Need* It or Do We Just *Want* It?

(published in *LA Progressive* on 15 April 2020)

We all remember Mom or Dad asking us, "Do you really *need* that or do you just *want* it?" Our leaders don't seem to understand that when we say we need programs like Medicare for All, we aren't spoiled brats throwing a tantrum because we can't get the shiny toy Becky down the street has. Do we *want* Medicare for All? Of course we do. But that's because we *need* it.

If we ever needed proof that tying health insurance to the workplace is a bad idea, it's during a pandemic killing tens of thousands of people and hospitalizing even more. Right as more than 16 million Americans lose their jobs—and any health insurance that came along with it, the presumptive Democratic nominee for president is dismissing universal healthcare as a fundamental right. But those 16 million workers aren't the only Americans without healthcare. Their children are without it now as well. *And* the 30 million others who are *already* un- or underinsured.

My sister, a nurse in a nursing home, doesn't get health insurance from her employer. She hasn't had health insurance in years. Does she *want* medical coverage or does she *need* it?

While Medicare for All might be the most obvious need Americans have, it's certainly not the only item on our ~~Want~~ Need List.

Almost every other industrialized nation in the world offers their citizens (and even many non-citizens) tuition-free college. Here in the U.S., we tell prospective students that if they want an education bad enough, they need to take out a student loan that may sink them in debt for thirty years. If they want to be low-life bums, though, without any education or vocational skills, that's their choice, and they need to live with the consequences. The question for our political leaders is this—Do we as a nation *need* forty million uneducated adults in the workforce or do we just *want* chronic unemployment and poverty? A follow-up question might be—Do we *want* to deal with the consequences of having that uneducated workforce or have we simply created a society where we *need* to?

Do we merely want to reduce carbon emissions or do we need to?

Do we need to incarcerate a larger percentage of our population than any other nation or do we just want to?

Do we need a voting system that disenfranchises large portions of the electorate or do we just want one?

Do we need a homelessness crisis or do we just want one?

Do we need to separate the children of asylum seekers from their parents or do we just want to?

Do we want clean drinking water or do we need it?

We have made choices as a nation that answer every one of these questions and more. We've chosen to create ignorance and poverty. We've chosen to perpetuate illness and misery. We've chosen to create and maintain economic injustice, racism, and sexism. Those conditions didn't just "happen." We *made* them happen.

It's all too clear that Republican leaders don't want to address these problems, but by consistently pushing pro-corporate, anti-worker policies on us, Democratic leaders tell us time and again *they* don't want to address them, either. They understand that they need to give lip service to solutions, that they need to make token advancements, but they don't want to adopt policies that would all but eliminate them.

As voters, we don't *need* Bernie Sanders or Elizabeth Warren or Alexandria Ocasio-Cortez or any other specific person. What we do need are humane policies. DNC leaders, you need to hear this: you can give us whatever candidates you want, but if you don't give us the solutions and programs we need, *you* need to understand that there are political consequences.

You should *want* to avoid them.

COVID Blankets for Poor People

(published in *LA Progressive* on 26 May 2020)

Most of us were never taught in school that European immigrants—priests and preachers and other generous donors—often gave blankets to Native American communities to promote peace and goodwill. Blankets that sometimes were intentionally infected with smallpox. If God chose to kill off hundreds of thousands, even millions, of "savages," those sinners had no one to blame but themselves. Yet even if many Christians today were never taught this well-documented history, they seem to understand the process instinctively. They refuse to release approved funding to Native American communities dealing with the coronavirus. They supply them with malfunctioning equipment or items they haven't requested instead of the supplies they need. Some people even point their fingers and say, "If you don't like it here, go back to your own country." While specifics of our long tradition of hatred may not be widely taught, hate itself is taught in America every day—by the most righteous among us.

We teach in school and at church and in the media that we can't provide universal healthcare to our citizens because doing so would be immoral. We've provided people with decent jobs so they can pay for their own healthcare. If those jobs are in crowded meat processing plants where they must work next to hundreds of coworkers infected with COVID, that's hardly our fault. God clearly established capitalism in the New Testament as the only humane way to run a society. Jesus spoke of it frequently, as did John the Beloved. It was Judas who spoke all the time about socialism. We bear no responsibility for handing out disease-infected jobs to the poor.

It's not like we *hate* the lazy and weak. Every day on TV, we announce our gratitude for grocery store cashiers, for Amazon warehouse workers, for bus drivers, for certified nursing assistants. They're our heroes. We do flyovers to thank them. It's not *our* fault if their employers don't make their workplaces safer. Just because we wash our hands of the problem and don't demand safety measures.

Besides, this "pandemic" is way overblown. It's clearly a plot to make Trump look bad. We all know that Democrats are part of the Deep State. Nancy Pelosi waving a flag looks like a vampire holding a cross. AOC goes to fancy hair salons. These people control the lamestream media that keep telling lies. Yes, some old, decrepit patients are dying a few weeks early, but Democrats are using inflated death tolls to hurt the middle class. The fact that tens of thousands of people are dying in other countries around the world, even in places like Brazil and Russia that are controlled by strong leaders, just shows the depths to which Democrats will go to hurt America.

Atheists are *praying* for people to die.

Of course, it's all China's fault.

Though the disease isn't very serious.

But those people eat *bats*. And chickens. And dogs.

They eat dogs in Vietnam, too, and South Korea. And in Switzerland. The Swiss even eat cats.

Asians are so disgusting.

Trump is the greatest president we've ever had. It's not *his* fault he threw out the National Security Council's pandemic response handbook that had been written during Obama's presidency. Barack *Hussein* wasn't even American, not even Christian. It's not Trump's fault he was forced to fire scientists and appoint political friends to lead the agencies we need during a pandemic. Scientists are godless. The whole reason we're being punished with all this suffering and death in the first place is because so many liberals have turned away from God.

Not that there's much death and misery actually going around. No more than usual with the seasonal flu. That can be cured pretty easily with Jim Bakker's silver solution or by injecting ourselves with UV light. If worse comes to worst, we can always let Kenneth Copeland blow on us.

It's all Hillary's fault, anyway. She should be in prison.

And everyone knows this fake "crisis" was the idea of a commie Jew to prevent Donald Trump from holding rallies. He's in cahoots with Pocahontas. Bill Gates just wants to implant chips in everyone to track us. That's why we need the government to monitor everybody's emails.

Because Big Government must be brought to its knees. And *we* should be the ones to do it, not China or Canada or Germany, because no one understands that our political system is the absolute best in the world more than we do.

"COVID-19 or COVID-1984!"

"Scamdemic!"

"Give me liberty or give me COVID-19!"

"Let my people golf!"

Even though we try hard to be loving, caring Christians, when we see reporters covering our protests—protests we're *entitled* to because of the First Amendment—we can't help but yell and curse them when they arrive wearing masks. How disrespectful! Trump should just shut down all those lefty organizations that keep spreading so much fake news. It's *their* fault there's such division in our society. We're patriots when we rip masks off stupid people or push them into ponds or cough on them or wipe our noses on their sleeves. We're really justified in doing pretty much anything we want because these infidels are deliberately hurting America. They're traitors who must pay for their treason.

Why else would we bring Confederate flags to our rallies?

"If ballots don't free us, bullets will!"

"No Room for Fascists!"

It's intellectually dishonest for Democrats to suggest the swastikas on our signs represent *us*. When we wear KKK hoods at a rally, we're making a point about *you*.

Democrats are making the virus *political*. Just when we thought they couldn't get any more despicable, they use photos of mass graves to try to manipulate people.

Thank God those are just bodies of dead crisis actors.

So we'd better go out and buy some more guns. We may have to eat our neighbors.

The Constitution gives us the right to go into any store we want without a mask. The same way business owners have every right to put up signs declaring "No Shirt, No Shoes, No Service." The same way bakers can turn away degenerate gays. If perverts want to buy a wedding cake, they have the right to go somewhere else. *We* believe in freedom of religion. People *we* refuse to serve have the God-given right to leave us alone.

But we demand the same freedom in return. By definition, Christians can't discriminate. Yet those corrupt Democratic governors won't even let us go to church. That alone proves they're secretly Satan worshippers, which we've suspected all along. We should be able to gather with all our loved ones, sit next to each other for hours singing and praising God, which we can't possibly be expected to do at home as a family. We should be able to go to work without masks, fire our employees who arrive wearing the offensive things, turn away customers who try to come into our businesses wearing such infernal objects. It's a plot to let black people rob our stores, a plot to make everyone wear burqas. As law-abiding citizens, we should be able to go into any workplace or business we want without wearing masks.

Everyone's trying to make us follow goddamn rules all the time! We're supposed to be "PC" and not kill anyone. We simply won't have it!

We'll make the rules.

And those rules are that Trump is always right. Democrats are always wrong. Scientists and doctors are *usually* wrong, unless they agree with Trump. This isn't rocket science, after all. Above all else, we must preserve Wall Street because without it, we'll never be able to enter heaven when we die. If some poor people die, or ignorant workers, or Native American heathens, who are we to tell God how to do his job?

We're Christians. We put God first. He took this land from Tonto and gave it to *us* because we deserve it. We must do everything we can to avoid worshipping the anti-Christ. No mark of the Beast on *our* foreheads. That's why we proudly wear our red baseball caps made in China proclaiming "Make America Great Again."

It's sad, isn't it? Truly, genuinely sad, that everyone else is so terribly deluded. But we're not spiteful. All that we do is guided by love. So we are more than happy, always, to send everyone heading to the mortuary our sincerest thoughts and prayers.

The Religious Right and Right-Wing Death Panels

(published in *LA Progressive* on 25 May 2020)

When the Affordable Care Act was up for a vote during President Obama's first term, the cry from right-wing opponents was that "Obamacare" would create "death panels." Bureaucrats would sit in meeting rooms deciding if Grandma got to live or not. Socialized medicine, which the ACA is not, would be even worse. Only capitalism cares about Grandma's life. It wasn't true then—as insurance execs sat in meeting rooms determining which patients would receive treatment and which would be left to die—and it's certainly not true now as right-wing "Re-open the economy!" advocates prove.

Several of my religious friends have strongly criticized temporary workplace closings to flatten the curve during the early part of the pandemic. Two of them, both physicians, characterized the situation as "destroying the economy to save old people who would have been dead in two weeks anyway." But that rationale, even if it were accurate, raises an important religious/political question: if we don't care about those last two weeks of Grandma's life now, was it OK before the pandemic, and will it be OK again afterward, for families to euthanize Grandma when it looks like she's getting close to the end? And if it *is* OK, would its acceptability be based on pain and quality of life or would it be based on economic concerns?

One can't always tell if an 81-year-old is going to die in the next few weeks. She could live another ten or fifteen years. Valerie Harper (Rhoda from *The Mary Tyler Moore Show*) was diagnosed with lung cancer in 2009. Would it have been OK to write her off then? She was still alive in 2013, when the cancer spread to her brain and she was given three months to live. Surely, at that point, it would be OK to consider the remainder of her life meaningless. "No one's giving up a haircut for you!"

But in 2016, she was still working on film projects. She did not die until the end of August 2019.

So at what point would it have been acceptable for Valerie to willingly choose physician-assisted death on her own behalf? At what point would it have been acceptable for her family to decide that for her? And if neither she nor her family had that right, why do Republicans feel entitled to claim it for themselves, magnanimously sacrificing the lives of people they don't even know? After all, they can hardly limit the sacrifice to their own parents, regardless of how much they might stand to inherit. They are making this decision for *everyone*.

If suicide is a sin, why doesn't the religious right put up a fuss when they hear an elderly person offer themselves as a sacrifice to the economy? Is someone else's suicide only acceptable when it benefits you? Why do so many of the faithful pressure the old and sick to willingly give up their God-given right to live a decent life for as long as they can?

Recently, a right-wing pundit said he was willing to eat his neighbors and feed them to his children if he had to. His superpower, he boasted, was honesty. What he didn't add was that this push to "Re-open the economy!" while unprepared means he's also willing to throw 100,000 additional grandmas into the maw of corporations just to briefly assuage their insatiable hunger.

Of course, Americans of the religious right don't want to kill the old and sick themselves. They just want to "let" them die. They want "nature" to "take its course" so life can go on...for the people who matter.

If this was just an either/or proposition, perhaps they might even be right. But it isn't. We could choose to send monthly checks to every worker until the pandemic was under control. Such a program would cost less than the trillions given to corporations. And even if we insisted on giving money primarily to these corporations, we could still choose to make the bailouts contingent on corporations paying their employees. There are a variety of other options to explore as well.

But for the religious right, sending someone a check just for sitting at home not infecting anyone is a sin far worse than senilicide, worse than euthanizing the disabled, worse than terminally ill patients requesting medication to allow them the luxury of dying painlessly on a timeline of their choosing.

No, the only moral course of action is to let Grandma, and Grandpa, and Aunt Sally, and Cousin Joe suffer for three weeks on a ventilator before dying. If healthcare professionals also get sick and die, or bring it home to their family causing some of their loved ones to die, well, they all knew what they were getting into when they applied to nursing programs and medical schools. And if hospital custodians get sick and die, too, no one forced them to get a job at a medical facility. Besides, it's not a sin to let poor people die naturally, is it? That's just "life."

If "the economy" is more important than the lives of anyone who "might" die in the next few months or years, why not just kill everyone outright who reaches the age of 65 or 70? No one needs to battle over Social Security anymore. Think of the money we could save by not wasting it on these mostly unproductive people. And that's just their pensions. There are tens of billions more to save every year by no longer wasting medical treatment on people who are doomed to die relatively soon no matter how much we spend on them.

We might as well round up and euthanize all the homeless people, too. Think of the millions we could save, how lovely our cities could be without them. Pretending that all human life deserves equal respect is just a big waste of money. Even worse, it's inconvenient.

Americans are happy with politicians who dedicate a trillion dollars a year to the military because that outrageous expense will "save lives." So why does money matter *now* to save our most vulnerable? Do we only stand up for others when it's easy?

We don't have to sacrifice the economy to save the most vulnerable in our community. We don't have to sacrifice the most vulnerable in our community to save the economy.

We might, however, need to sacrifice corporate welfare.

That's a death panel we should all want to be on.

Securing the Well-Being of Citizens is Not Tyranny

(published in the *Salt Lake Tribune* on 23 May 2020)

A former missionary colleague of mine explained that he believes both those on the right and the left want basically the same thing—to help people—but his beef is that those on the left want to achieve it through tyranny. If "the government" assists the poor, the rest of us are forced to pay higher taxes. Helping is only appropriate if the behavior is performed without coercion. It was "Satan's plan" to *make* people be good. God instead chose to give us free will. But everyone, both on the right and the left, should *want* the state to improve the lives of all its citizens.

During the current pandemic, many insist that requiring people to wear masks is heavy-handed government interference. And yet some Republican business owners deny their employees a choice by firing them if they wear a mask to work. It's economic tyranny if "big government" orders businesses to close temporarily to avoid spreading the virus, but it's not a problem if Republicans order them to reopen and immediately rescind unemployment assistance to workers who must now choose between homelessness and serious illness. A "stay at home" order to protect the public during a crisis is a violation of the First Amendment, but routinely monitoring emails and phone calls without a warrant under normal circumstances is "for the greater good" and so doesn't violate the Fourth Amendment.

Republicans claim that using tax dollars to provide everyone a college education is tyranny. But requiring every pacifist to financially support the military is no more than "responsibility." Demanding we share the burden of providing healthcare to all is a prescription for losing our souls. But compelling everyone to gift fossil fuel corporations with billions in subsidies is a divine cure for the economy. It's a sin to use a single penny of taxpayer money on abortion but it's "free will" to force women to bear the children of rapists.

My missionary colleague and I spent two years of our lives volunteering to teach others about Mormonism. But even among Mormons, free will isn't entirely free. No one is *forced* to pay ten percent of their income to the Church, but if they don't, they can't marry in the temple. They can't attend their children's weddings. They can't enter the Celestial Kingdom after they die. Our culture determines the "natural" consequences to every free choice, in order to elicit the behavior we want.

To quote Dana Carvey's Church Lady, "Isn't that conveeeenient?"

As citizens of a civilized nation, we make a social contract. If it's not tyranny to use taxpayer money to hire police officers and firefighters to protect the community, it's not tyranny to use taxes to hire doctors and nurses to protect patients. If it's not tyranny to use tax dollars to teach a child to read, it's not tyranny to provide an adult adequate job training.

Many on the right firmly believe in enforcing the policies that complement their religious or political agenda. They only protest—carrying assault weapons into state capitols as a show of "force"—if those policies make compulsory helping people they feel no compulsion to help. Grandma might die? She's so old she'd be dead in a couple of weeks, anyway. And it's not like we're condemning her to hell. She'll go straight to Paradise. Desperate asylum seekers might die in detention camps? Well, we can't help *everyone*. The truly empathetic would understand that those folks are better off in Spirit Prison where they'll finally be open to accepting the gospel.

Working together to improve the lives of all members of our society is not tyranny. It's our civic duty. It may well be the purpose of religion to help perfect our souls, but the job of the state is to secure the physical well-being of its citizens. If those on the right feel that obligating them to treat others humanely is a sin, the rest of us are free not to accept their conclusion.

But those of you on the right needn't worry. Rest assured that if you're forced against your will to protect workers, or give the unemployed an education that allows them to support their families, or stop corporations from polluting the environment, God can always punish us later for helping you.

Do Extremists Just Want to Kill People They Don't Like?

(published in *LA Progressive* on 29 April 2020)

Washington state lawmaker Robert Sutherland (R-Granite Falls) took part in a protest at the state capitol in Olympia, calling for an armed rebellion if he couldn't go fishing as a result of the stay-at-home order. I understand the concern over economic hardship caused by social distancing to slow the pandemic and try to give people the benefit of the doubt in regard to their motivations. But the more I watch how these extremists at "let us get sick and die" protests behave, I think all they're really looking for is a chance to "defend" themselves. Many on the far right have been talking about "second amendment solutions" for years. They don't want to go fishing or go shopping. They want to kill people they hate and are trying to make it look like self-defense.

I think of police officers who shoot unarmed motorists and then plant a gun on the body. I think of "good neighbors" who start a fight with someone "suspicious" and then "have" to kill that person in self-defense. Yes, not all officers are horrible. Not all neighbors are wannabe killers. But some are. And the evidence accumulates daily that these extremists who want to "liberate Minnesota" and "liberate Michigan" and "liberate the country" are driven more by hatred than the desire to see a movie at the theater.

If all you want is to see a movie, why are you waving a Confederate flag while you protest? If all you want is to go bowling, why are you shoving and beating journalists who are simply recording you exercising your First Amendment rights? If all you want is to go fishing, why are you threatening to kill your colleagues at work?

I'll admit, there are some people on the far right who I don't like, a few I might actually hate. But I don't spend my days coming up with ways to justify killing them. I hope to reason. I hope to persuade. I hope to rally enough voters who are open to reason and persuasion to vote. But I don't look for opportunities to kill.

When it first became apparent that ICE detention centers were going to be overrun by the virus, concerned citizens began demanding that asylum seekers be released. But I knew it was never going to happen. Those on the right might never say it publicly, but many of them are *happy* the families they've put in concentration camps are going to die. Some will act deeply offended and scream their denial, the way they pretend Trump was only joking about shooting up bleach. We all know the truth, but we're pressured into believing we've signed a social contract to keep pretending we don't. So even if the offensive comment is true, perhaps "civility" dictates an apology on my part.

The same civility that has right-wing politicians keeping people imprisoned as the virus spreads through the camps. Sure, a few children are released, a few parents are deported, but tens of thousands of human beings remain trapped as the infection spreads.

"Leaders" throughout the country are also "working on" ways to release non-violent offenders from state and federal prisons. And as they "try" to "work out" the details, the infection rate at some prisons has already reached 75%.

Because really, though no decent person would say so out loud, this virus is serendipitous, a *perfect* way to get rid of so many people those on the right don't like.

You know, like the black and brown people in major cities—and on reservations—who die in disproportionately high numbers. Sure, we'll get around to providing tests and ventilators and treatment eventually, but let's allow the riff raff to die off first. We can just say it took longer than we'd hoped to get ourselves organized. Better yet, it was those stupid Democratic governors who couldn't get their act together. If anyone's to blame, it's *them.*

Anne Frank wasn't "murdered" during the Holocaust. She died of typhus, as did her sister Margot. Was it really the fault of their captors that these teenage girls got sick? Disease is simply a part of life, after all.

It's hardly natural, though, if you deliberately create the conditions where the disease can kill those you don't like in massive numbers.

People say that love is blind. But it turns out that hate is blind, too. Some of these extremists are so driven by their hatred they can't grasp the fact that many of the people they love will also die because of their actions.

The right-wing lieutenant governor of Texas said, "There are more important things than living." And he's right, at least as far as these extremists are concerned. And that more important thing…is killing.

I only hope that for the rest of us, there are more important things than complaining. Or pretending.

Like organizing, striking, protesting. And voting.

Consistent Messaging in an Emergency

(published in *LA Progressive* on 18 May 2020)

The oxygen masks drop down from above our seats. I hadn't paid attention during the pre-flight emergency spiel. I'd heard it all a thousand times before, and the flight attendants weren't singing or dancing to keep it interesting. A couple of hours after take-off, I'd looked up from the book in my lap to clear my head. *Guns, Germs, and Steel* wasn't light reading. And I'd seen two attendants whispering worriedly to each other, one of them pointing at a window or something near it. I couldn't see anything suspicious and went back to my reading as one of them picked up a handset and whispered into it.

A minute or two later, the loudspeaker crackled and the captain began speaking. "The Fasten Seatbelt sign is on. We may run into some minor turbulence, but don't be alarmed."

And that was that. The flight attendants smiled cheerily, if a bit plastically, and encouraged a few passengers to buckle up. I felt a little unnerved when one of the attendants closed his eyes and mouthed something to himself, but then he smiled again, and I went back to my reading.

And then the masks fell. Passengers are shouting out questions now as the tubes dangle before us. An elderly couple two rows ahead scream in terror, immature old people. One of the flight attendants grabs her headset and orders the adults in the cabin to put on oxygen masks before helping our children. "Or you may pass out before you can help your child."

"Oh my god!" someone else screams. I'm already tired of the melodrama.

Just as I begin pulling the elastic bands behind my head, the captain comes over the loudspeaker again. "Please stay calm. The oxygen masks deployed accidentally. We are in no danger. If you feel any shortness of breath, it's because you're overexcited. Calm down and breathe normally."

I can hear nervous laughter from the passengers near me, mixed with angry accusations. One middle-aged man across the aisle punches in a nasty text to the airline. A young woman kisses her daughter's hair ribbon, telling the girl not to worry. My heart is beating so fast it hurts. My son starts crying because I'm squeezing his hand too tightly.

Looking out the window, I see that we're descending slowly. We're going to be OK.

The "Fasten Seatbelt" sign goes off. An elderly man stands and heads for the bathroom. Who knew there were so many old people?

"Please take your seat immediately!" a flight attendant yells at him.

"But—"

"There's a crack in the window!" the flight attendant screams. She's quite unprofessional.

Obviously, if there were really a problem with the oxygen level, we'd all be unconscious by now, so the emergency must be overblown. Surely, the captain knows more than these flight attendants, who are really no more than glorified waiters and waitresses. Why would a crack cause all the masks to fall?

Someone just pushed an emergency button when they didn't need to. A passenger might have had a heart attack because of this reckless behavior. I'm appalled. I pull out my phone to send a stern text to the airline as well.

But my phone is ripped out of my hand when the cabin experiences explosive decompression. The elderly man flies down the aisle along with the flight attendant yelling at him. Books and laptops zip past, hitting passengers on the head, tearing off a piece of someone's forehead here, a tuft of hair there.

I grab my oxygen mask, fumbling for it in the wind and panic, barely managing to cover my face before I see my son slumped over in his seat. My heart pounding harder than ever, I slip his mask on, and after what seems an eternity, he slowly begins to stir.

There's no point dragging the analogy out any further, especially since no analogy is perfect. But the one thing anyone trained to handle an emergency knows is that consistent messaging is important. Even as a cashier, I'm trained by my employer in First Aid and CPR. One of the first steps is to take control of the situation. We don't look around timidly and say, "Anyone want to call 9-1-1?" We point to someone and order them. "YOU, call 9-1-1! And YOU, wait by the curb to wave the medics down."

If it turns out that in an actual emergency, we're too emotionally shaken to perform as we've been trained, we can practice later to be more prepared the next time. But if after three months of daily practice, we still can't make it through an announcement without changing our mind in mid-sentence, or becoming so flustered we simply turn around and walk off, I think it's clear this is not something we're ever going to be good at. It doesn't mean we're not great at a hundred other things, but leading in an emergency is obviously not one of them.

Even if we're generally inclined to trust captains over flight attendants, I hope we can all agree that at the very least, we need a new captain, one who doesn't deny the reality of what's happening aboard the plane he's piloting. Assuming we survive the current catastrophe, we can stick with the same airline next time or move to one of several competitors, but for God's sake, let's choose a captain who isn't going to kill us.

Please Contact Me When You Have a Platform Worth Supporting

(published in *LA Progressive* on 12 May 2020)

Because I donate to progressive causes and candidates, I end up on a great many email lists for other candidates I've never heard of. One of them emailed me recently, informing me he was progressive and asking for my financial support. His email didn't reveal much of his agenda—the assumption was that I'd just hand over my money simply because he claimed to be one of the good guys. But when I checked him out online, I discovered that despite good policy proposals on climate, he did not support universal healthcare. I emailed back and explained that while I found him overall to be better than most Democratic candidates across the country, my finances were limited, so I could only donate to those who met all of my minimum requirements. His lack of support for a national health program was a deal breaker.

I'd been polite in my email, and the candidate replied in a similarly non-confrontational manner. "I believe in offering my constituents a choice," he said, "so I think Medicare-for-All-Who-Want-It is the best solution."

He's not the only candidate to say something along these lines. It *sounds* reasonable but it really isn't. I grew up in a right-to-work state in a religiously and politically conservative family. As a teen, when I heard about right-to-work legislation on the news during dinner one evening, I announced emphatically, "No one should be *forced* to join a union."

My father, a contractor who'd spent the previous twenty years building houses, wasn't impressed. "If you don't belong to a union," he told me, "you have less job security and you make less money. And if everyone else on your job site belongs to a union, whatever benefits you do get are because *they're* paying all the dues while *you* contribute nothing."

During Obama's presidency, I saw the same dynamic in the debate over the individual mandate for the Affordable Care Act. The difference there was that the premium was 30% of my monthly income, hardly "affordable." A law can't successfully force someone to hand over money they can't earn. The system was designed to fail.

Which is a similar problem facing the post office. Congress has deliberately made it impossible for the US Postal Service to succeed. It *had* been one of the most successful government programs in history. But if we sabotage it, of *course* it won't function adequately. Then pro-corporate politicians can say, "See? The private sector can do this better."

It's not uncommon for a failing company to hire a new CEO "to turn things around." All too often, though, the company's failure by this point is unavoidable. So a woman or an ethnic minority is hired for the position, and when the company does finally go under, everyone can say, "See? Women [or blacks or Latinxs or Asians or whoever] just aren't good at business."

Britain's National Health Service was one of the best in the world until recently, when politicians began turning pieces of it over to private corporations. *Now* it's become less efficient. All a set up so that pro-corporate leaders can say, "See? Socialized medicine is a failure."

Even Medicare for All in the U.S. would struggle as long as pharmaceutical companies and medical supply companies remain for profit.

We have no problem awarding billions in bailouts to corporation after corporation. Money for FedEx but not for the post office. Money for drug companies but not for a national health program. "That would be an abuse of taxpayer dollars!"

Odd how our "principles" only kick in when politicians can no longer direct funds to their corporate donors.

Many CEOs accept bailout money and then continue firing hundreds, even thousands, of employees. As Robert Reich regularly points out, "Billionaires aren't going to save us."

Private prisons give corporate owners an incentive to encourage long sentences for minor offenses, even to label some behaviors criminal that shouldn't be. The way some unethical dentists keep finding "issues" with a patient's teeth, performing one unnecessary procedure after another to keep the money coming in. The way an untrustworthy mechanic can keep finding "problems" with our car engine. The way weapon manufacturers are incentivized to promote war.

Democrats like to point out every conflict of interest President Trump or Mitch McConnell or other Republican leader has.

But when profit is the goal, every system, as well as every leader in it, has a built-in conflict of interest.

Is capitalism too big to fail? Perhaps. But it's definitely too profit driven to succeed.

Money is power, and corporations have most of it. The challenges we face to reach economic, social, and climate justice are overwhelming. The least we can do—and often the most—is direct our limited funds and energy *only* to those candidates and causes which meet the minimum requirements, and demand accountability when we do.

I emailed the politician who'd contacted me one last time. I didn't want to sound snarky, and I suspected my note would be interpreted in that tone, but I meant my comment sincerely. "When you finally have a platform worth supporting, please contact me again."

Zero is Not an Increment

(published in *LA Progressive* on 11 May 2020)

Moderation is a virtue. Compromise signals maturity. Reasonable people vote for centrists. Working across the aisle is the only way to pass legislation in Washington. In a fiercely divided Congress, incremental change is the best we can hope for. But to all those who complain that progressives are asking too much too quickly, I'd like to point out that zero is not an increment.

The claim of success would be false, even if incremental change was in fact taking place. But all that "realistic" Democrats have gained us lately are *fewer* Supreme Court judges, *fewer* district court judges, *fewer* appellate court judges.

"It's not our fault!"

And yet Democrats blast Republicans for never taking responsibility for anything.

The last Democratic president ordered *more* deportations than his predecessor. In the first two years of Obama's presidency, Democrats controlled both houses of Congress as well as the Oval Office. And yet couldn't even muster the courage to put single-payer healthcare up for a vote. Virginia is currently led by a Democratic governor, a Democratic House, and a Democratic Senate, giving Dems the power to do virtually anything they want. Yet, according to Oxfam,

Virginia is still 51st out of 50 states plus the District of Columbia in the arena of workers' rights.

51st place out of 51. The incremental advance there is zero, as it is in far too many places on far too many issues.

Remember the episode of *I Love Lucy* when Lucy and Ethel bottle their own salad dressing? They tell Ricky and Fred they're making money, but it turns out their profit is just three cents per jar, "and that three cents goes to Caroline Appleby" for getting them an advertising spot at her husband's television station.

"But we'll make it up in volume," Lucy declares bravely.

Basic math quiz: what is 3,957 times zero?

I remember a particularly dry summer in Mississippi during my early teens, when everyone's corn crop was shriveling in the heat. One afternoon, I told my dad excitedly, "It's raining!"

He looked outside and gave a dismissive grunt. "Not enough to do any good."

I didn't understand. Surely, a little water was better than no water, right? But my father was correct. While technically a five-minute light drizzle isn't "nothing," its effect *is*. "Something" has to mean more than a trace, it has to mean "something that changes the outcome in a meaningful way." .034 inches of progress isn't "zero" but it may as well be.

When criticizing Republican distortions of the truth, Democrats like to quote Nazi propagandist Joseph Goebbels— "If you tell a lie big enough and keep repeating it, people will eventually come to believe it." Those terrible, dishonest Republicans.

And yet Democrats keep telling those of us on the left a Big Lie as well: "Keep voting for us and we'll finally get you what you want. I know it doesn't look like it right now, but you have to look at the bigger picture. We're working behind the scenes for you. Just trust us a little longer. Only 10 or 20 years. It's not forever. We're really trying. Have patience, and little by little, we'll save you. As long as you keep the faith and stop complaining. Complaining will destroy everything we've accomplished so far."

Explaining that what we need isn't what we've been given is apparently more powerful than Democratic legislation, stronger even than Republican opposition. Those idiots who demand the capacity to pay their rent are the real reason we don't have more progress.

Odd that complaining about Democratic inaction is bad but complaining about progressive goals is just fine.

The federal minimum wage, adjusted for inflation, is lower now than 50 years ago. From 1968 through 1974, the minimum wage was $1.60 an hour, which as of January 2020 was equivalent to $11.65. The actual minimum wage in January 2020 was just $7.25. That's -$4.40. I suppose a negative number is an increment, if we don't mind going in the wrong direction.

But has there really been *no* progress in the past several decades? Of course there has. A black man can now become president. While a jogger can still be shot just for being black. Lesbians can get married. While a woman impregnated by a rapist is still forced to bear the child. *And* grant the father partial custody.

When an energy revolution is needed immediately to limit greenhouse gases to levels that keep large swaths of the planet even marginally inhabitable, an incremental approach to lower emissions by 2050 just isn't going to cut it.

No human society will ever be perfect. But it's not unreasonable to expect more in the U.S. than we currently have. Other nations have had universal healthcare for 70 years. Some have had tuition-free college for decades as well. If Democrats still can't provide these basic needs for us after all this time, do even measurable increments really matter?

Might that be the reason more and more people give up and vote for Independents and Democratic Socialists and the Green Party and, when profoundly desperate, even someone like Trump?

The claim at election time is always the same. We're facing an emergency. We need to get the terrible Republicans out first and *then* we can worry about moving forward later. But a rallying cry of "We can't do anything just yet but we honestly intend to one day" isn't effective, even *if* it were true. And, finally, by small increments over many years, our faith in empty promises has grown too large to ignore.

If Democrats want to lead, they must take us where we actually need to go.

Politics as Religious Conviction

(published in *Main Street Plaza* on 7 June 2020)

The religious right is ramping up for a modern-day crusade. That's not a metaphor. Racially motivated killings are in the news every day. Homophobic and transphobic murders are committed regularly. Poor men and women are forced to work in conditions that *will* kill a significant portion of them. When the first few drops of rain fall on a sidewalk during a thunderstorm, we initially see individual wet spots before us, but the dry spaces between them shrink rapidly, and after only a few minutes, the entire surface is covered. We don't need to conduct a violent pre-emptive strike to acknowledge the urgency of making political change while we can. Every election is touted as the "most important" of our lifetime. We're trained to dismiss such claims as emotional manipulation, which they often are, but the danger we face now isn't theoretical. It's real and growing stronger every day.

Last night, I watched Henry Gates on PBS as he revealed the fate of the extended families of Jeff Goldblum, Terry Gross, and Marc Maron during WWII. The phrase I kept hearing was, "and that's when further details vanished from the record" as each family's community was obliterated, one after the other. The program airing afterward told the story of the Pittsburgh synagogue where 11 worshippers were killed, just days after their latest active shooter training. I watched a survivor of the Jewish deli shooting in Paris take a self-defense course while the widow of one of those murdered happily recounted her courtship and marriage. She seemed surprisingly well-adjusted, till the moment in the story where she had to talk about that terrible day.

Yet perhaps the worst segment of the program was the summary of how a former hero, a Holocaust survivor who rose to extreme wealth and then donated almost 80% of his fortune to charitable organizations, was recast as an evil Jew trying to take over the world. George Soros was turned into a scapegoat in Hungary so a dictator could consolidate power.

Then I watched as the Labour Party in the UK embraced anti-Semitism, pushing its many Jewish liberals out of the party.

As I watched these disturbing events onscreen, my husband sat in his office in the rear of the house, enjoying a weekly Zoom meeting with friends. After rejoining me in the living room, he told me that a group of racists had hacked into their gathering, shouting the N-word over and over until the one black woman in attendance signed out. After several minutes, the admins regained control and blocked the intruders, but the incident left everyone shaken. It was hardly the first time the black member of the group had faced such language. It was just the first time some of the white folks in the group had felt they were under attack as well.

As ex-Mormons, my husband and I were both raised to believe blacks were morally inferior, that they'd been "less valiant in the pre-existence before we came to Earth." Even now, *decades* after we left the Church, when we see a black driver ignoring a crosswalk or a black pedestrian tossing a piece of trash on the sidewalk, for a split second, maybe only half a second, we think, "What can you expect from someone like that?" Many of us who are happily ex-Mormon have moved past the unhealthy lessons we've been taught, yet even hearing current LDS leaders insist all people are equal regardless of the color of their skin doesn't *entirely* erase all the former teachings still clinging tightly to the neurons that code our memories and deepest beliefs.

How much worse is it for those who are still trained every day by their religious leaders to consider any other group of humans "less than"?

The latest killing of an unarmed black man by the police in Minneapolis was all over Facebook the past couple of days, yet not a single person in my family commented on the death of George Floyd. One family member several years ago had posted "Police Lives Matter!" in response to a previous incident, but other than that, I've seen nothing posted in regard to any of the dozens of killings that have made it into the news since then. My relatives live in the Deep South, where I grew up as well. I remember my parents buying me a Confederate cap and a rebel flag to play with when we visited the Civil War memorials in Vicksburg, where at least one of my ancestors had fought. My mother would say, "Skip this monument. These are Yankees. Oh, here's a good one. One of *ours*."

My mother was a genuinely wonderful person in almost every way. But she was infected by the hatred she'd been taught her entire life. When we describe those folks saying and doing racist things as bigots, however accurate the label, they are *unable* to see themselves or each other as such because what they *can* see is that they're "nice" people in so many other ways. You know, the "fine" people at the rally in Charleston who chanted "Blood and soil!" as they marched with other neo-Nazis while a young woman was murdered by another right-wing extremist.

Most of my religious friends treated me wonderfully...until the day they learned I was gay.

But these right-wing folks are all on the "same side," so they treat *each other* well, they're nice to *each other*, they're "good people" in their own and each other's eyes. We're angry when they demonize us, but they are just as angry when we demonize them, because they honestly cannot see the harm and suffering they cause.

Is that really possible?

The evidence before us suggests that it is.

A vegetarian might well worry about the pain steak lovers cause the animals they slaughter, but do vegetarians consider the possibility a plant might not enjoy being chopped down and eaten, either? Perhaps a plant isn't truly able to feel pain the way animals do, but the point is that we don't even consider the possibility. It's simply not part of our mindset. Does that mean we're heartless and cruel to cucumbers?

Of course, our *absence* of concern for the feelings of vegetables isn't the same as the *presence* of a powerful animosity toward others that often exists in the hearts of the religious right.

The Civil War isn't ancient history for people in the South. Many white folks have passed on their anger, generation after generation, at having lost the battle to keep their slaves. Their anger isn't only over losing the war, the way a petulant child might be upset over a game of checkers. The loss is an overwhelming message sent directly into the deepest reaches of their psyche that they aren't superior to blacks as they'd claimed. That idea of superiority is such a core belief that losing it is like hearing you're a pod person from *Invasion of the Body Snatchers.* "No! *They're* the pod people! *I'm* human! I'm one of the good guys! I *am!*"

They tell themselves this every day, every time they see a news story about a black criminal, every time they see a black person in public say something "rude," every time they hear rap music. In many ways, their behavior is the same as that of news anchors who every single day point out something awful Trump has said, concluding with, "Can we now all finally agree that Trump is terrible?" The possibility that even one person in the audience isn't yet convinced threatens their conclusion, and they *must* believe they are right. So they spend every day "proving" their point over and over and over again.

Such emotional neediness is unappealing no matter who is doing it, but right now, most of the physical danger is coming from those on the right. If a black person does better in life than they have, it's because the black person received an unfair advantage. If a Jew does better, it's because there's a secret Jewish underground. No one who isn't a white Christian should be doing *better* than they are. If someone is, it can only be because he's stolen what rightfully belongs to whites. And thieves must be punished.

This incredible lack of self-confidence may seem pathetic or even laughable, but the desperation and simmering anger it creates is real, and it's being stoked by the unscrupulous to gain power. And just as a virus doesn't recognize borders, neither does hatred. It has spread to every region of our nation. White supremacist groups exist even in the most liberal states.

In the wake of the most recent police killing, a black church was burned in Mississippi, with the words "Vote Trump" spray-painted on the brick wall outside. Of course, we all know Mississippi isn't a liberal state. We *expect* this kind of thing in the south.

That's a problem. This isn't a "new" normal *there*. We cannot allow it to become normal everywhere.

White protesters armed with assault weapons rallied in Minnesota at the capitol recently to protest stay-at-home orders yet faced no repercussions. When unarmed men and women gathered to protest the unprovoked killing of George Floyd, they were met with riot gear and tear gas.

Even now, with a photo of the police officer kneeling on George Floyd's neck until he suffocated to death posted next to a photo of Colin Kaepernick kneeling in protest before a football game, I see empathy-challenged people insisting, "Two wrongs don't make a right," as if killing someone and protesting the killing are not only equal, but also both wrong.

Yet those actions *are* equal to them. If a black person has "attitude," he deserves to be killed. Not shunned. Not chastised. Not fired. *Killed.* An equal response to the "offense." And the very *existence* of blacks, gays, Jews, Muslims, Native Americans, and many others is the offense that cannot be forgiven.

The violence isn't caused merely by a few crazy people on the fringe. It's perpetrated and perpetuated by those in uniform and elected officials in office. It's the institutions themselves that are problematic, as well as all the "regular folks" who accept these killings as "understandable." Most of my right-wing friends and family aren't actively committing these atrocities. They simply don't care a great deal if they happen. Even those who feel the police did "something" wrong have a hundred priorities higher on their list.

Like same-sex marriage. And atheists. And people saying some of the most dreaded words in the English language: Happy Holidays!

And, of course, the abortion doctors who "murder" millions of babies. Because to the religious right, there is *no difference* between a fertilized egg, a zygote, a morula, a blastocyst, an embryo, a fetus, and a baby. Explaining the science is meaningless. They *know* anyone who doesn't agree with them is a murderer. Murderers, clearly, should be put to death. And while there may be no difference between a zygote and a newborn baby, there's *plenty* of difference between a murderer and an executioner.

This isn't a case of semantics. It's not theory. It's *truth* to them, and someone who bases their decisions and behavior on these kinds of truths are left with few options.

If *you* had to vote for either a repulsive man who fondles women and makes fun of the disabled *or* an intelligent woman with no known scandals *but* who will install judges who ensure that millions of babies will be not "aborted" but *murdered*, what *to you* is the lesser of two evils?

We like to call those on the religious right hypocrites, and certainly many of them are, just as many are on the left (shout-out to the latest "Karen" in Central Park), but in the mindset of a religious conservative, these two candidates aren't even close. One is bad and the other is very, very, very, *very* bad.

Unfortunately, "understanding" where they're coming from doesn't eliminate the danger we face. If anything, it helps us realize we're not worrying about a non-existent threat.

A man in the Reopen North Carolina protest said he was willing to kill to fight against the New World Order, and that such killings of fellow Americans wasn't terrorism. For most right-wing protesters, it's the unquestionable will of God.

They *mean* it.

In my Baptist high school, we used to sing, "God said it. I believe it. That settles it for me."

Rolling our eyes is not an appropriate response. Almost all of us make fun of these extremists, even knowing it's counterproductive. I do it, too. It's difficult not to. But these devout believers are serious about their convictions, and they've become more and more emboldened over the past few years.

To paraphrase Condoleezza Rice, "We don't want the smoking gun to be a mushroom cloud over the ACLU." Over a Jewish community center. Over a gay nightclub.

When people tell us they hate us, we should take their word for it.

At a neighborhood park a few days ago, while admiring the beautiful rhododendrons and brilliant hummingbirds, I could also hear the repeated "bam bam bam bam" from a police association shooting range nearby. It's a sound I hear from my front porch every day, something I never quite get used to. Since I live across the street from a school, I dread the day I might hear that sound from twenty yards away. When my husband attends far-left political meetings a few neighborhoods over, I worry about the sirens I hear in the distance.

Two elderly women chatted with me at this neighborhood park last week, from a reasonable distance, about how most people were being pleasant and cooperative in the effort to keep the park safe. When they saw a couple of people blocking the path to take pictures, the women waited patiently for them to finish. Then a man in the group turned to the women and held out his phone. "Would you take a picture of us?"

The women deferred, saying they'd rather not risk infection. The man, who'd been friendly a moment before, now saw them as enemies and hissed, "For something that's no worse than the flu!?"

The women, both elderly, were shocked. "People die of the flu," one of them said. "And even if you don't die, it's miserable. So even *if* COVID were no worse, I wouldn't want it."

But the man was furious, enraged, full of immediate, irrational hatred.

It's become a religious conviction for those on the right that Democrats are using the coronavirus as an excuse to deprive Republicans of their liberty. We're not talking politics anymore—we're talking religion. And when someone feels they're morally superior, that others are morally inferior, and that God wants the righteous to destroy his enemies...well, let's just say *Where Angels Go, Trouble Follows*.

As a Mormon missionary, I felt I had been called as a *Saturday's Warrior*, chosen to "gather the faithful" in the Last Days. Those of us sent to Rome talked about the awesome responsibility of being sent to "Satan's doorstep." A friend who was assigned to Portland just months after Mt. St. Helens erupted felt thankful that Heavenly Father had prepared the sinners in that area by "sending them a message."

I was shocked to discover that one of my missionary colleagues was a Democrat. Of course, he'd converted to the true church as an adult. He didn't know any better. Still, I thought, it was surprising he'd been found worthy to serve a mission.

Months later, another missionary colleague suffered a nervous breakdown. When we knocked on doors and the occupants of the apartment would tell us calmly they weren't interested in our message, my companion would turn to me after the door closed and address me as if I were the occupant. "You're not interested!? Not interested in your own salvation!? You're not interested in being with your family after you die!? Not interested in following the Savior!?"

I had learned by this time not to take rejection personally. If people were interested, great, we'd teach them. If they weren't, that was their decision. I didn't need a complete stranger to validate my life.

But my companion did. He took a stranger's disinterest in his religion as a *personal affront*. An affront to his intelligence, an affront to his two-year sacrifice, and an affront to God himself. This emotional reaction was so severe he was barely able to function.

I know two men who ended their friendship because one thought Daniel Craig was a great James Bond and the other thought he was ugly.

But what's happening in politics isn't funny, it isn't "stupid." It's not "worrisome."

By their very nature, political parties are opponents. What's changed in the last few decades is the growing conversion of politics into religion. It's deadly enough when one Christian religion demonizes another—think of the Reformation in Europe, the Spanish Inquisition, and the situation in Ireland. But when Republicans see Democrats *literally* as the party of the Devil, it's not just ridiculous. It's *dangerous.*

An elected official in New Mexico recently announced, "The only good Democrat is a dead Democrat." A police officer in Louisiana bemoaned the fact that more blacks hadn't died in the pandemic. These aren't just "feelings" and "opinions." They are votes. They are policies.

They are gun owners.

When someone says they want you dead, believe them.

For the religious right, gays were responsible for Hurricane Katrina. Gays and Jews were responsible for 9/11. Gays and Jews and Bill Gates are responsible for COVID. Except, of course, when the Chinese are responsible.

In the mid-1990s, I converted to Judaism and was active in the community for several years. It's been a long while since I identified as a Jew (I see myself as a Mormon Jewish atheist) but I remembered my time as a Jew fondly and kept two mezuzot affixed to the door frames of my bedroom and office. I never nailed one on the front doorpost, always aware that announcing Jewish affiliation could be problematic. It's the same reason I never pasted pro-gay bumper stickers on my car.

A few months ago, I removed the two mezuzot inside my home. It's not that I'm "afraid to stand up" for the Jews any more than I'm afraid to stand up for gays or any other oppressed group or person. I simply realize we're not in a period of "rude" discourse. Right-wing politicians have been pushing hatred for so many years that now, with the pandemic providing more fuel, this nation has become a drought-stricken, desiccated forest.

Maybe *most* people of every political persuasion are good, but it only takes one idiot to toss a lit cigarette into the brush. And once that conflagration begins, we'll all be caught up in the disaster that follows.

We see the irrationality of those on the right every day but don't want to accuse anyone of plotting our literal destruction. It might "raise tensions" or "lower the level of civility." And just as some whites can't entertain the horrifying notion that they might not be superior to others, the rest of us find it too frightening to consider that our lives might legitimately be at risk. So we convince ourselves that this is all rhetoric and policy, quite bad enough though not cataclysmic.

Then last night, I heard Terry Gross wonder if she would have known when to leave if she had lived in eastern Europe just before the outbreak of WWII. Would she have gotten out? "When's the right time?" she asked.

It's not a rhetorical question.

In *The Day after Tomorrow*, the character played by Dennis Quaid urges the scientist played by Ian Holm, "It's time you got out of there."

The scientist replies sadly, "I'm afraid that time has come and gone, my friend."

For better or for worse, we're here and we're not going anywhere. Let's do what we can to help each other survive.

I sat on my porch this morning so I could listen to the bees buzzing about the California lilac.

But all I could hear was gunfire from the shooting range somewhere on the far side of the park.

All or Nothing Racism

"White people are racists."

"How dare you judge me! *I* never did anything to you! *My* ancestors weren't slave owners! You saying that white people are racist *is* racist!"

To reduce this kneejerk reaction, racial equity trainers often rephrase the culprit in the opening statement as "white dominant culture," with the caveat the term doesn't condemn *all* white people. Although members of the white dominant culture are quick to understand that *some* white people doing bad things doesn't mean all white people are bad, many of them seem unable to make this same cognitive leap when considering the actions of others.

The reality that *some* protesters are violent, that *some* participate in looting, shouldn't mean that *all* people protesting injustice are bad, or that the issue being protested isn't valid. Those who defend the police after yet another unprovoked killing rush to point out that not *all* officers are bad, that it's not fair to cast them all as racist, but the same concession is rarely offered in return.

Does the fact that this or that Republican was caught beating his spouse mean that all Republicans are abusers? Then why does the fact that this or that Democrat was caught committing insider trading mean all Democrats are white-collar looters?

A legitimate problem in our society is "Republican dominant culture." Individual Republicans, perhaps many of them, are clearly good, well-intentioned people. But just as a "good" white person is obligated to actively work to break down structural racism, a "good" Republican must work to tear down the racist (and sexist and homophobic and xenophobic) parts of Republican culture. Not to do so is to perpetuate the oppressive behavior of others, which at best makes the "good" person an accessory to oppression. Are accessories to murder, even third-degree murder, truly eligible for the label "good"?

"Good" Democrats must stop supporting candidates and policies that oppress workers. They must stop their "unhappy acceptance" of bills that help fossil fuel corporations continue escalating the climate crisis. They must stop being accessories to the dismantling of the postal service, to the denial of healthcare to millions of Americans, to foreign policy that oppresses hundreds of millions of people all over the world.

If "it's complicated" is an excuse for any inhumane policy or position, perhaps we should just abandon all pretense, both to ourselves and others, that we're good.

Some people embrace their power and corruption. That's certainly a choice we can make. But if we do sincerely *want* to be good and honorable, then we must stop taking everything personally. If someone on "our" side does something unacceptable, we say so, demand accountability and, when possible, restitution. If someone on the "other" side does something commendable, we acknowledge it. If someone on either side has a legitimate grievance, we don't suppress discussion but address the problem.

It should not be up to others to audit our dominant culture. Because it *is* our culture, we may be blind to its faults, but once they're pointed out, it's to our own benefit to fix them. If we've moved into a majestic home in a beautiful, established neighborhood and spent several years and tens of thousands of dollars renovating the house, and then some random neighbor stops by and says, "You know, I can see from the size and position of that crack in the foundation that your front porch may fall off during a heavy thunderstorm," lashing out in anger and ordering the neighbor to leave won't alter the facts.

Blaming the subsequent collapse on the neighbor when we retell the story may help us deflect the blame, may help us feel better about our poor choice to ignore the warning, but it doesn't resolve the problem.

Some socialist organizations have homophobic policies. Some environmental groups have leaders who commit sexual improprieties. No political party, no organization, no religion can be free of members who do bad things. When we excuse bad behavior and harmful principles in the dominant culture we inhabit, when we let things slide, when we agree to be silent partners to oppression, we are not being good people.

So let's suck it up, let's demand accountability and change within our own groups, and let's stop being accessories to the brutal crime of tribalism.

Back Yard Politics is Destroying America

What happens when "Not in my back yard!" turns into "Not in my country!"?

No one wants a garbage dump in their community. The most "law and order" people among us don't want a prison in their neighborhood. The most humane don't want a homeless encampment in theirs. No one, rich or poor, liberal or conservative, wants an oil pipeline or fracking well a quarter mile from home. This natural self-interest has always been problematic, as the privileged ensure their own comfort while foisting the unpleasant side effects of our culture on the most vulnerable.

But what happens when the "toxic waste" voters don't want anywhere near them includes people with dark skin? What happens when it includes LGBTQ folks, refugees, immigrants, people who worship differently? Most importantly, what happens when the leaders these voters elect follow through on the unspoken truth they've heard loud and clear—America's "back yard" is the entire country, and there's *no* acceptable place anywhere in our nation for those they consider human trash?

People with a conscience can't allow themselves to actively "eliminate" people they deem unacceptable...but they *can* rationalize voting for someone who will do it for them. "No one's perfect," they say, "and he has other policies I like." But they're not particularly worried when Japanese Americans are interred in concentration camps, when AIDS sweeps through gay communities, when Indigenous women are raped and murdered in record numbers. They're OK with COVID-19 disproportionately killing blacks. If Latinx families are separated, imprisoned in dangerous conditions, and eventually deported back to even more dire circumstances, it's no concern of theirs.

What happens when a majority of Americans, or at least a majority in states most privileged by the Electoral College, *want* all these groups to "go away"?

We keep telling ourselves that *our* country could never devolve into fascism and dictatorship. But then we creep ever closer to Argentina's corruption of the late 1970s and early 80s, when up to 30,000 dissidents and human rights activists "disappeared."

We all want to live in Utopia. Mormons tried out the United Order, a Finnish man in Brazil created Fazenda Penedo, and Jim Jones established Jonestown. Some of the more than three dozen <u>American experiments</u> were more successful than others, but even when we see failure after failure, we keep trying because we all want something better than we have now. Even the most privileged among us, who should already have everything they want, still want more. This longing is not just a personal or cultural need; it's almost certainly rooted in our DNA.

But whatever its source, one thing that history has shown us time and again is that oppressing, imprisoning, and exterminating those we see as obstacles to our idea of Utopia is never the solution.

We worry that elections are useless, that there is widespread voter suppression and voter fraud, that paper ballots are destroyed, that voting machines are rigged or hacked. We worry that even if the candidate we choose ends up winning, in the end it will make no difference that is both meaningful and positive.

We can be sure, though, that *not* voting *will* make a difference, an extraordinarily meaningful one, and it most definitely won't be positive.

Both intellectual and human purges are deadly, even when in support of lofty ideals.

Whatever our personal goals for the best life we can lead, each of us should want to cleanse from the neighborhood we call America all elected officials who consider other humans, even many of their own supporters, as no more than troublesome weeds infesting their dictatorial back yard.

We must remember that remaining "neutral" by abstaining always favors the oppressor. Let's commit to vote so we can clean up our neglected front yard.

What if the Current Administration is only the Warm-up Act?

Ever since I came out as gay in the 1980s, I've kept my passport up to date. I always understood that LGBTQ folks had little security, that I might have to flee at a moment's notice. All forms of gay sex were felonies in Louisiana back then. And I knew it was a rare oppressor who made an appointment for the exact hour he was coming to arrest you.

On August 27, 2005, I discovered I had thirty minutes to pack. Because I'd been distracted with the other turmoil in my life—my husband had just died of cancer, I'd been forced to find another place to live, and I'd been transferred at work to a new location I didn't like under a new manager who enjoyed assigning busywork—I hadn't paid much attention to the storm brewing in the Gulf of Mexico. But now Katrina was a Category 5, and I needed to leave immediately.

I grabbed my prescriptions, two changes of clothing, my resumé, and my passport. Then I headed out of town.

I never saw my apartment again.

In December of 2019, I sent an email to a Canadian bank. "What would I need to open an account?" I figured it might not be a bad idea, given the deteriorating political climate in the U.S., to put a thousand dollars aside in another country…just in case. It turned out I'd need a Canadian-issued ID. I hated the idea of traveling to Canada just to get the ID, which would almost certainly not be processed on the spot, requiring me to make a separate trip later to open the bank account.

And I was embarrassed to tell anyone I was making this contingency plan. I might be a hypochondriac, but I didn't want to be a drama queen, too.

So a few more weeks passed. Inertia isn't only a principle of physics. It's also true in psychology. Still, I knew I couldn't put it off *too* long. The von Trapp family escaped Austria *one day* before the border closed. I remembered the harrowing ordeal Betty Mahmoody faced escaping Iran with her daughter, the horrors of the Underground Railroad in the American South, the East Germans killed trying to get across the Berlin Wall. And I couldn't forget the terrifying ordeal a Czech circus troupe endured escaping over a bridge into Bavaria. Hell, even in the wake of Katrina, black New Orleanians were stopped at gunpoint when crossing the Mississippi River Bridge to reach dry land.

Then news about the novel coronavirus started popping up. Boarding a bus to Canada might be risky now. I was already worried about taking public transportation every day, but at least I wasn't in close quarters for three full hours with a potentially contagious seatmate. Perhaps after things died down, I could finally take care of the new account. With mainstream media campaigning against Sanders and even Warren, the hope of defeating Trump in November seemed less and less likely. I looked up some bus and train schedules, debating how to broach the subject with my husband, who hated using money frivolously.

Then the pandemic hit in full force. I lost one of my part-time jobs and was in danger of losing the other. Had I already waited too long to establish my contingency plan?

A few days later, the border closed.

Since then, the political atmosphere in the U.S. has only grown more volatile. Protesters with promoting White Supremacy, with signs asking for "fags" to be killed, started rallying in public and posting threats online. Trump ramped up taunts against reporters. Hate crimes, already on the rise, increased even more. Protesting fossil fuel projects became felonies. Convicted Trump associates began being released from prison. Trump and Pompeo seemed to be pushing the country toward war with Iran. I realized that if the presidential election was "postponed" in November, or if its results were tossed out, democracy in this country wouldn't survive. It may already be too seriously injured to recover. Investigators and department heads and inspectors general have been dropping like flies for the past three years, and not from a virus.

Though corruption is contagious. As is fear.

Perhaps we've all waited too long to act.

But if any of us makes a comparison to Hitler or the Nazis, we're instantly shamed for doing so, our arguments automatically dismissed as hyperbole. Trump's a buffoon, we're told, not a mastermind. But people *are* dying. They *are* being locked up. People *are* losing everything, and that all started well before the first case of COVID-19. Stalin might be a less problematic example of dictatorship, but too few Americans know enough of the details for the comparison to be effective. Even fewer are aware of the atrocities committed during China's cultural revolution.

Years ago, when I first accepted the permanence of my sexual orientation, I understood that instead of coming out publicly, I could lead a secret life, not letting anyone at church know, not letting my family and straight friends know, not letting anyone at work know. But I already grasped the emotional damage such a life would inflict. While I realize everyone's situation is different, my choice was to tell *everyone*. I wrote letters to politicians, to Church headquarters in Salt Lake, to my local newspaper. I wanted to make sure I was on the FBI's list so that if things ever did get worse for gays, I'd know I couldn't "pass" but would have to fight.

This was the period when senators in DC were suggesting people with HIV be quarantined permanently from the rest of society. Right-wing pundits were demanding gay men be tattooed. Tens of thousands of people were dying because it was "inappropriate" to spend "tax dollars" on HIV research.

As a Mormon, I'd grown up with the concept of a "year's supply." We were routinely taught there would be hard times ahead and we needed to be prepared. At the Baptist high school I attended, we were taught about the Rapture and its accompanying seven years of tribulation. The message of future crisis was a dominant part of my upbringing. That was almost certainly one of my motivations for reading Holocaust literature as a teen. I wanted to prepare myself emotionally for what lay ahead.

I was going to be one of the survivors.

A rabbi once told me the Shoah could never happen in America.

I'm no longer a believer in any god. But I remember an Auschwitz survivor from the synagogue I attended. I remember the Rwandan genocide. I remember the "disappeared" from Argentina. I remember that one of my high school classmates was a huge fan of David Duke. Every year, I can see the steady increase in gerrymandering, voter purges, elimination of polling stations. I see reports of "glitches" that shift every vote for a Democrat into a vote for a Republican. I see how easily many of my religious family members dismiss police killings of unarmed blacks. Despite slanted coverage by the media, I can see what's been happening to Palestinians my whole life, can see what's happening in Syria right now, can see what's happening to African refugees in overcrowded boats off Italian shores.

After relocating to Seattle in the aftermath of Katrina, I eventually found a decent job as a bank teller. One day, a woman came up to deposit a check into an account for the Freedom Socialist Party. I was a little unnerved as she threw in some casual but clearly proselytory remarks about socialism while I conducted the transaction. I'd heard my entire life how awful socialism was, and although I'd already moved from Republican to Democrat to progressive, this pro-Trotsky indoctrination made me uneasy.

And the woman kept coming back to conduct more business. She was pleasant enough, though, and even invited me to a Christmas party at her home. Having been unable to make many friends in the seven years since I'd arrived in Seattle, I decided to attend with my husband. The activist had mentioned she might need some carpentry work done, and my carpenter husband needed the work.

He ended up joining the FSP, and I began attending occasional events with him down at "the Hall." I did temp work with Radical Women, a group that also met in the same location. I proofed articles for the *Freedom Socialist* newspaper. I took part in some rallies and protests.

And every time I did any of these things, I knew my participation was being recorded by *someone.*

I can't write legibly enough anymore to keep a handwritten journal, so I type it in a Word document. Yet if I save a copy to myself in an email, the next day, I start seeing ads pop up on Facebook for something I've never discussed with anyone, that I've only ever mentioned in my journal. The idea of every communication being examined seems preposterous, but at the very least, attached documents are being scanned for keywords, most likely by corporations, not "the government" (though I admit the distinction is fuzzy). One time, I didn't even write anything anywhere, only had a brief discussion with my husband in the living room during a commercial break in the show we were watching. And two hours later, ads and articles about the subject started popping up on the sidebar in my email. These weren't generic, popular topics. These were targeted ads.

Whenever I talk on the phone, whenever I shoot an email to a friend, whenever I look up something online for a story or essay I'm writing, I'm aware it's all being tracked.

I'm not a fan of conspiracy theories, despite my evangelical upbringing. A friend of mine has suffered for the past thirty years with schizophrenia. I understand enough about delusion to question myself.

But just as we're shamed not to compare the growing fascism in our country with Nazism, we're gaslighted from believing we're being monitored. The story set in East Germany, *The Lives of Others*, could never happen *here*.

The Mormon Church keeps files on dissidents or, as they label us, "apostates." I know members who were assigned to keep tabs on other members. I remember the spies sent to record license plates outside of gay bars in Salt Lake, the students coerced to submit to electroshock "therapy" or be kicked out of school.

When President Trump announced during a press briefing recently that he was taking hydroxychloroquine, my husband suggested Trump's doctors were probably only *telling* him that's what he was taking so he'd shut up about it. I joked that maybe his doctors were secretly the ones pushing it on him just so they could legally administer something that might trigger a heart attack.

And as soon as I said it, I thought, "Will I be arrested now for 'threatening' the president? In my own home, in a private conversation? From a completely powerless position?"

Perhaps not every worry we have these days is justifiable, but I do wonder if it's already too late to save ourselves from the next round of concentration camps and mass murder. Sobibor and Manzanar and Wounded Knee and the killing fields of Cambodia aren't fables and myths from the distant past. And more articles appear every day warning of the growing threat of the extreme far right.

When I was young, I made plans for how I might survive when things "got bad."

I've had to accept that I'm not going to survive.

But I want Mayim Bialik to survive. And I want David Hogg to live. And Melissa Harris-Perry. And the neighbors who stand six feet outside my front door and ask if my husband and I need them to pick anything up for us at the store.

Donald Trump cannot be re-elected. In our dysfunctional two-party system, the Democratic nominee becomes our only viable choice. We can stick with Biden or work in the remaining time before the Democratic convention to push another nominee. We can debate the best strategy, but we need to acknowledge that an oppressive leader doesn't always spark a "revolution." Sometimes, he and his oppressive successors just continue oppressing…for decades, even centuries.

Like many others, I want to tune out, stop watching the news, hunker down, and try to survive emotionally during this stressful time. But that's exactly what allows ruthless people to gain power. We need to work on saving our democracy as if our lives depend on it. Because one way or another, they do.

Social Media Anger Management

With reduced hours at work, and performing more of our work from home, many of us end up lingering too long on Facebook. We connect with friends and family we can no longer visit in person, and someone is always posting a funny cartoon or cat video. But I find that spending more than a few minutes on this social media platform makes my day worse, not better. A recent study shows that bots and algorithms drive division amongst us, not only between the left and the right, which would be bad enough, but also between the subgroups within each category. Despite its benefits, a platform like FB contributes to more grief, anger, and despair than to comfort or solutions. It's like AZT in the early days of the AIDS crisis, helpful and toxic at the same time. It will be better for us—personally and for society in general—to reduce our intake.

Social media etiquette alone is exhausting. When I read a post linking an article about animal abuse, how do I respond? Do I hit Like because I'm glad my friend acknowledged the problem? Or does that sound like I'm pro-animal abuse? When I read a post about suffering children in Syria, will my Love be interpreted as sadism? The story of an increase in homelessness makes me sad, but when I hit the Cry emoji, my friend subsequently posts his disappointment that everyone isn't hitting the Angry emoji. I actually do want to hit Angry on multiple posts but doing so makes me feel I'm contributing to a growing tension that can't possibly end well. And, frankly, it's exhausting being angry about *everything*.

Where's the goddamn Disgust emoji?

I like posting links to songs and comedy bits. I love posting pictures of beautiful libraries and majestic trees. But I feel that people will find such posts frivolous during a global pandemic and growing political oppression here and abroad.

Then there are the challengers. "I bet no one reposts this."

Yep. You're right. I'm not going to repost that when you try to force me. If you post something worthwhile, I'll repost it without coercion. You gain nothing by being self-righteous.

So much virtue signaling to wade through day after day.

Like this essay.

I don't have the energy to fact check every post, so sometimes, I won't even hit Like because I'm afraid I'm perpetuating misinformation. Then when I do post a link to a Snopes refutation, do my friends think I'm being helpful or just an ass?

If I stay away from FB for a day or two, I almost always feel better emotionally, especially if I'm also limiting cable news. But does disengaging mean I'm letting bad guys get away with murder? Can I effectively push for positive change if I'm uninformed on the multitude of essential stories circulating every day? Is being depressed and unhappy the price of being committed to justice?

When I'm gone for a while, I worry that my friends feel slighted I haven't Liked or Angried more of their posts. They'll think I don't agree with them on this or that important point.

If I comment on someone's post rather than simply hit an emoticon, the poster is just as likely to misinterpret my response as appreciate it, even if I think I'm saying something supportive. As far as "discussing" topics with those who hold differing views, that only leads to bitter feelings and routine Unfriending. I suppose it must happen, but I've never personally witnessed anyone changing their mind in one of these battles.

One of the worst kinds of posts, though, is the Zinger. Somebody posts a meme saying something pithy that skewers the position of opponents. Perhaps it's genuinely funny. But unless people are tailoring who receives those posts, the self-satisfaction they bring us can't make up for the damage it does by further alienating people with other views, even those on "our side."

And for God's sake, can't some enterprising business person offer an effective, low-cost service to proofread the damn things? Even the Zingers I'd be willing to post are filled with typos and grammar errors. "Illiterate? Write for free infomration!"

Finally, there's the moral dilemma of supporting an organization and CEO whose politics and power create serious problems nationally and even globally.

So I'm limiting my exposure to the toxic atmosphere that on some days I contribute to as much as anyone else. Fifteen minutes a day. That's it. I encourage others who can to do the same.

But first, you've just *got* to watch this short video. I promise it's worth it:

<u>This teacher's COVID-19 song made our hosts cry with laughter.</u>

Things to Say to Police While Being Murdered

(published in *LA Progressive* on 3 June 2020)

The white governor of a small Mississippi town dismissed George Floyd's claim that he was being suffocated. "If you say you can't breathe, you're breathing." We heard the same thing when Eric Garner was choked to death for the violent crime of selling loose cigarettes. Technically, the claim is true. A person does need some degree of air flow to be able to speak. But is it fair to expect someone facing imminent death to be 100% scientifically accurate? "Officer, I believe you are increasingly obstructing my air flow by 14.2 percent every 33 seconds, and at this rate, my red blood cells will be unable to provide oxygen for my brain within the next minute and 48 seconds. Give or take ten seconds. I'm afraid I left my oximeter at home."

Since police officers are unwilling to accept "I can't breathe!" as a motivation to stop their assault on an unarmed suspect, perhaps we can come up with a list of better options for those of us being killed.

"You're killing me!"

I'm not sure that expression would work, though, despite its simplicity. I keep hearing my mother's voice. "Stop crying or I'll really give you something to cry about!" And we need to avoid exclamation points. Police officers don't like suspects with attitude.

How about, "I have an underlying medical condition that your assault is aggravating. I may stop breathing or go into cardiac arrest if you don't desist."

OK, we're back to that "I can't breathe!" awkwardness again.

Perhaps a gentle reminder? "Passing a counterfeit $20 bill doesn't carry the death penalty, even if a jury of my peers does decide I'm guilty, *after* a trial, *and* a conviction."

People who are being killed should also keep in mind other phrases we can substitute into this template: "going five miles over the speed limit," "being a scofflaw," "hanging out with friends." We can laminate a card with this information and carry it around in our wallets, review it during quiet moments so we'll be able to recall the necessary phrases for specific occasions.

We can even role play with our loved ones. The family that practices being murdered together stays together.

Another option is to wear a T-shirt every time we step out of the house—even if everyone else at our workplace wears business attire—with one helpful phrase on the front and another on the back. We can include the alerts in two or three languages to recognize the multi-cultural make-up of our police force. Light-skinned folks might consider easily readable tattoos on their arms, their necks, even their heads if they're the type who like shaving off their hair or have managed to reach the age when they naturally start to go bald.

Obviously, the safest course of action is to *never* commit any infraction of any kind ever, under any circumstances. We might stand a better chance of not being choked to death, but if we hope to protect ourselves against other forms of killing, we still need to come up with another set of phrases we can shout

out at a moment's notice. When we're asleep in bed and police officers shoot us eight times in the middle of the night, we don't have a lot of time to explain that drug possession is another of those crimes that doesn't carry the death penalty. It's an especially difficult sentence to blurt out since we don't even know why we're being shot. Or who the police are even looking for. What phrase are we supposed to use? Just start making random guesses?

A friend did try a sign on his front lawn that read, "You've got the wrong house," but then the mail carrier stopped delivering his mail.

He placed a different sign on his bedroom door, using luminescent ink. "There might be someone in here you're not expecting." But then his girlfriend got mad and dumped him.

These things are just so complicated. Maybe we should do a study. Come up with a task force.

Perhaps if we can save a little money by shoplifting, we could afford some kind of surgically-implanted device that would respond to unnatural pressure on our airway or critical blood supply and automatically shout out the appropriate alerts to any police officers killing us without *our* needing to say anything at all. The offending officer might be more open to criticism if it wasn't coming directly from us.

I'm sure we'll eventually come up with a workable solution. We can't realistically be expected to come up with good answers overnight.

It's not as if we've known about this problem for more than a month or so.

Or a year. Or twenty years. Or fifty. Or four hundred.

Does Anybody Here Know
How to Fly a Plane?
(published in *LA Progressive* on 7 June 2020)

On April 28, 1988, Aloha Airlines Flight 243 lost 18 feet of its roof in mid-flight, killing a flight attendant who was sucked out of the plane, and seriously injuring another flight attendant and seven passengers. An additional 60 passengers sustained minor injuries. Pilot Robert Schornstheimer, a former flight instructor, had created simulator exams for his students that encompassed multiple crises. A few students complained that so many things would never go wrong at the same time in real life. But Schornstheimer and his co-pilot, Madeline Tompkins, faced more than immediate decompression of the plane and the loss of the cockpit door. The noise of rushing wind was so loud they had to communicate through hand signals. They were unable to reach the one flight attendant still conscious, who was also unable to contact them. The horizontal stabilizers were seriously damaged, the vertical stabilizer partially damaged along with both wings. They were unable to deploy full flaps upon their emergency landing, forced to attempt the landing at a higher speed than normal. And they were unable to confirm if the landing gear at the nose of the plane had descended or locked into place.

The two pilots landed the plane successfully, such an astonishing feat that it was later turned into the movie *Miracle Landing*. As I watch the multiple crises facing America now, hanging on for dear life as I stare at the gaping hole where a protective roof used to be, I remember what happened over the Hawaiian islands that day in 1988, and I feel a glimmer of hope. A competent pilot can get us through this seemingly impossible ordeal safely.

Oh, wait.

And now I remember another film, *United 93*. Hijackers have taken over the flight. The passengers hear from their loved ones by cell phone what's been happening at the Pentagon and the World Trade Center. They know that if they have any chance at all to survive, they must take over the plane. They form a team, arming themselves with soda cans and whatever else they can find, a beverage cart, their courage, and their determination. They rush the cockpit.

And as they fight the hijackers for the controls, we see through the front window the green grass of a field in Shanksville, Pennsylvania approaching nearer and nearer.

Every time I watch the film, I keep rooting for the passengers. Maybe this time they'll succeed.

For some emotional relief, I watch *Airplane* and am struck by how often the nightly news makes me feel I'm living an absurdist comedy.

Whichever scenario we actually face in our nation today, we must remember that the conclusion isn't determined yet. Stowaway Helen Hayes could still live. Flight attendant Karen Black might manage to avoid the top of the mountain. Pilot Jack Lemmon might reach the surface of the ocean to call for help. We might be able to stand on the wings in the freezing Hudson River long enough to be rescued. If we aren't forced to eat our dead friends while trapped in the Andes.

Perhaps we should see ourselves as the crew of *Apollo 13*. If we can all work together, overcoming personality conflicts and lack of resources to repair the damage, we can still splash down safely and return to our families once again.

Maybe we'll even get to have attractive actors portray us one day in the film version of *Miracle Democracy.*

Ban All Routine Traffic Stops

(published in *LA Progressive* on 30 May 2020)

Dismantling institutional racism can't be completed overnight, but we *can* take steps to begin breaking off critical pieces right away. One easy yet essential advance is to ban traffic stops that don't involve immediate threats to public safety.

We've all seen the police engage in high-speed car chases in movies and on the news. Such chases are naturally exciting. But so many innocent drivers and pedestrians are killed as a result that some cities have banned car chases entirely.

People do not need to be injured or killed over minor infractions, not the drivers, not the officers, and certainly not bystanders.

Likewise, many routine traffic stops for a broken taillight or driving five miles over the speed limit end up with a police officer shooting an unarmed person, often someone black or brown. And these are drivers who *didn't* flee, who *didn't* pose a threat. But trained police officers are still human beings whose behavior can be influenced by fear and adrenalin. They are people who have grown up in a culture ensuring that even the most open-minded and humane among us have at least some lingering bias. When a life or death decision must be made in a split second, Sunday School lessons on "love thy neighbor" are replaced by the biological imperative to survive.

Are the officers justified in feeling this level of fear? Are they overreacting out of bias? Are they subconsciously—or even consciously—using the incident as an opportunity to hurt someone they consider "less than"? We can avoid these emotionally charged debates altogether. More importantly, we can avoid the deadly consequences of both justified and unjustified fear, of animus that can be lethal yet never proven. If police officers are legitimately putting themselves at risk by stopping a driver for something minor, that traffic stop doesn't need to happen. Let the errant driver go, for God's sake. Revenue from issuing tickets needn't drop. Unless there's an immediate need to stop a kidnapper or killer, officers can record the license plate (like cameras do at stoplights all the time) and mail a ticket to the offender. There's no point in a physical confrontation of any kind, even a mild, orderly one. Not being forced to spend millions on investigations and settlements, and not suffering constant PR nightmares, must surely be worth something as well.

If we can't justify endangering lives in a car chase over minor violations, then we shouldn't keep endangering them during traffic stops for non-threatening offenses. Such stops are not worth the death of the police officer, the driver, or any passengers in the car. Drug possession or car theft don't warrant the death penalty, after all, even after an arrest and conviction. Expired brake tags or carpool lane violations aren't felonies. These lapses certainly don't warrant execution without a trial. If "Police Lives Matter," why insist on endangering officers for trivial infractions?

And if "All Lives Matter," why feel compelled to continue a policy which can only lead to additional deaths of both officers and civilians over petty offenses?

As a child attending my first big tent circus, I remember the announcer revealing that the trapeze artists were about to walk across the tightrope without a net. Even at that young age, I thought, "Do they really need to risk killing themselves for a show?"

There are times police officers and other first responders need to put their lives on the line. There are times when everyday civilians need to do it, too.

But there's no need for anyone to risk their life just to reprimand someone over a broken taillight. Some officers have even pulled cars over simply because they were driving three miles *under* the speed limit along a corridor frequently used by drug traffickers. If the driver was being so careful not to attract attention, the officers reasoned, he was probably up to no good.

When officers can justify pulling over a car in perfect condition being driven without breaking even the most minor regulation, we have a problem with the status quo.

For the sake of those killed during routine traffic stops on a regular basis, we must cease all stops that don't involve reckless or intoxicated driving. "We've always done it this way" is no longer a valid rationale for sustaining a policy that inflicts so much unnecessary harm.

Let's ban all routine traffic stops.

Zip Ties and Apron Strings

In December of 2015, I started giving away some of my prized possessions. I didn't have many, mind you. But I loved reading middle grade literature: Enola Holmes, Sherlock's younger sister, who solves mysteries he can't; Theodosia Throckmorton with a gift for seeing which ancient Egyptian artifacts are cursed; Laura Ingalls recording the life of townspeople trapped inside during an interminable winter.

A few times each year, a young mother in my neighborhood stopped by with her young daughter to gift folks on our block with treats, and I decided to offer her the books I would no longer need. I didn't tell her I was planning to commit suicide. I simply said I no longer had space for them and thought her daughter might enjoy them.

The woman became convinced I was stalking her and refused to speak with me again.

The possibility that my actions could be so deeply misconstrued had never occurred to me. Frankly, I'd only been worried she might see through this well-known suicidal behavior and try to save me.

But we neither act nor react in a vacuum. Men are often predators and women are often targets. As a cashier, when I'm enjoying what I think is a casual chat with a female customer, I can tell the moment she begins to suspect the interaction isn't innocent. "Well, I guess I need to get back to my *husband*," she'll say.

"Oh, yes," I'll reply, hoping to relieve her worry, "I need to stop by the store for *my* husband on the way home." It never relieves her worry.

Even when women know I'm gay, they are often unable to keep themselves from seeing me primarily as a man, a leering, disgusting predator. To be fair, viewing unfamiliar men this way probably serves them well most of the time. But I was deeply hurt at a moment when I was already at my most vulnerable.

But when all was said and done, divesting myself of my favorite juvenile literature—my neighbor did take most of the books—still ended up a positive experience. I felt unburdened. Inanimate "things" can be comforting, but they also bestow an unavoidable obligation. They must be protected, preserved, dealt with. How do I make sure my books aren't damaged by sunlight coming through the window? What happens to that Val St. Lambert art deco vase during an earthquake? How would I ever manage to transport my wooden dinosaur carvings if I had to move to another home? What if the bank foreclosed and threw all of these precious items onto the curb? Even if I was unable to keep them myself, I didn't want them to just be thrown away. I had to protect this mini-Dresden from enemy bombs.

My personal library used to contain *thousands* of books. It's now down to seventy. In a perfect world, I'd have an entire room devoted just to the books I love.

But it's not a perfect world. It's not even a world, at least for the time being, where I can walk to the library and select another book to read.

When my printer died a couple of years ago, I chose not to buy another. For the few items I needed on paper, I could go to one of two neighborhood libraries or to FedEx.

Unless, of course, there's a pandemic.

Which brings us to healthcare, inexplicably tied to our employer, trapping us to our workplace because it's too dangerous to lose coverage when we leave.

In December of 2015 I was contemplating suicide for a variety of reasons, but the most immediate was a deep loathing for my job. I'd somehow ended up in a mortgage department processing equity loans. The workload was overwhelming, support from management was minimal, and more was being demanded of me every day.

The morning I woke up and thought, without hyperbole, "I'd rather die than go to the office today," I knew I had to quit.

I was HIV positive, with diabetes. I couldn't remain even moderately healthy without medical care. But what good is insurance, I asked myself, if I jump in front of a train? With only a few hours of guaranteed counseling, "coverage" was an anchor dragging me down, not a life preserver keeping me afloat. The need for income, obviously, was its own quicksand. The more my husband and I struggled, the more desperate our situation became. We might now lose our home. But when I was faced with the choice of daily misery to remain under a roof or daily misery from homelessness, I chose None of the Above.

My self-esteem was tied to my employment as well. It's difficult to feel good about yourself if you can't hold down a decent job. If you're not tough enough to stick it out. If you're not capable enough to overcome obstacles.

So I went from feeling suicidal to feeling even lower.

Yes, things *can* get worse. But it's almost always because we openly participate in our own bondage, believing that emotional and financial S&M is the sophisticated way to live. By definition, this behavior can't be an outlier if it's the norm.

We're tied to the desire for our parents' approval. My father was never impressed when I taught at a university. He wasn't impressed when I worked in a bookstore or at the library. For a few brief years, he was proud as I returned to school for a Biology degree so I could apply to medical school.

But when I didn't get in after several interviews, he went back to believing I was never going to do anything "worthwhile." And even if I didn't fully agree with his assessment, I was tied to it. Because mainstream society is also tied to it.

In the book, *The Object of My Affection*, the kindergarten teacher doesn't want to become a principal. He wants to remain a kindergarten teacher. But in the film version, he *must* become a principal for the movie to have a happy ending. To remain in such a lowly position would make the hero a loser.

As a bank teller, I wasn't permitted to feel content doing transactions at the window. My manager counted it against me in evaluations if I wasn't actively trying to "advance" to "the platform." The point of being a teller, he felt, was to use the position as a stepping stone to success—becoming a loan officer.

But I didn't want to become a loan officer. I wanted to be a good teller. And so I was marked down.

The Cowardly Lion in *The Wizard of Oz* boasts that he can fight with one hand tied behind his back.

Most of us must fight throughout our entire lives while handcuffed.

Decades after I left the Mormon Church, I married another ex-Mormon. When I met his brother, a former bishop and then a temple worker, I understood the high status he possessed. And still, when I learned he'd chosen not to serve a mission when he was nineteen, I was disappointed to find myself judging him.

We spend a lifetime learning familial, religious, and cultural expectations. And we're tied to them even when we don't want to be.

"You've lost some weight," I said to a friend I hadn't seen in a while. "You look good."

I'd meant it as a compliment, but aren't the accompanying unspoken words, "You sure looked awful before"?

Our self-esteem is tied to our appearance. It's tied to our education, to our income, to the prestige of our job or position in our religious community.

My previous husband was financially bound to a city he wanted desperately to leave. But his need to stay in a tenure-track position kept him trapped and too depressed to think of a way out.

One of my early boyfriends was rather "unfortunate looking," according to one of my friends, who assured me repeatedly, "You can do so much better." This friend, quite attractive himself, had been with his partner, also attractive, for many years. And his attractive partner beat him regularly. He'd been to the emergency room on more than one occasion and had the stitches to prove it. But he also "had his standards" and would never be caught dead with a man who looked like my boyfriend.

He was perfectly willing, of course, to be caught dead by his abusive "catch."

A close friend, this one another Mormon, was trapped in a marriage to someone she seemed at times to loathe. Her husband cheated on her on countless occasions and was obnoxious under the best of circumstances. When I asked during my last visit how he was doing, she said, in utter disgust, "He's still alive, isn't he?"

And yet she could not allow herself to consider divorce because that would mean she couldn't be with him for all eternity as a reward for her successful temple marriage. A temple marriage she somehow believed would be rewarded on Judgment Day despite her husband's repeated infidelity. A reward I couldn't fathom her wanting in the first place.

One of my husband's aunts clung desperately to life despite increasing health problems because she didn't want to be forced into her deceased husband's company again, her choice either to be trapped in an ailing body or bound in the afterlife to a man she despised. Prison now or prison later but always prison.

We're tied to the party line in politics, not allowed to dissent. Mitt Romney can be the Republican presidential nominee one day and shunned even by other Republican Mormons later for saying anything critical of President Trump. And Democrats can criticize Republicans for not allowing dissent while then lambasting any Democrat who steps out of line.

My second partner suffered chronic, debilitating pain and was prescribed OxyContin, but he had a difficult time getting what he needed. I read several articles and learned that opioids were only addictive if you took them when you weren't in pain. If you *were* in pain, the opioids addressed the pain instead of triggering addiction. I became an advocate for my partner, trying to get him the pain medication he needed. I didn't understand why he needed to shift to methadone.

Only years later did I learn that pharmaceutical companies had deliberately misled us.

It's mortifying to have been wrong about something that destroyed so many lives.

Almost all of us are bound by the need to save face. When new information is available and there's the possibility we must adapt our position, we often can't because we're afraid of admitting we were ever wrong to begin with. It's not enough to say, "When I know more, I make better decisions." We can't apologize for hurting others. We can't be happy we're progressing from bad to less bad to better to even better. We'll look weak, we'll look fickle, we'll look stupid. We'll have to accept that we may have spent twenty years defending something that in the end is indefensible.

A woman who left the Mormon Church in her sixties reported on Reddit that she felt those sixty years of life had been stolen from her. Some people would rather not have ten or twenty final years free of delusion. Better not to acknowledge the loss at all, to actively choose to remain deluded. Like chaining yourself in the basement, or inside Plato's Cave.

We're tied to the way things have "always" been done, unable to grasp that capitalism is no more a natural or God-given system than feudalism before it. We're trapped by either/or thinking. We either "reopen the economy and kill people" or "save lives and destroy the economy," unable to process any of the dozen other possibilities, some of which we can see in action in other countries leading the way. We either "hold people responsible" or "let them get away with anything." We see ourselves as either successes or failures, saints or sinners, supporters either of good government or oppressive policies. Those are the only options.

Worst of all, we allow all of these various cords to bind us to permanent submission against any action to save ourselves. We let ourselves be afraid of demanding healthcare as a human right. We let ourselves be convinced the only two options are corporate healthcare or single-payer, with socialized medicine too far-fetched to consider. We let ourselves be afraid to speak against the consensus of our peers. We let hundreds, thousands, millions of other people, most of whom we'll never meet, scare us away from being happy with our unimportant jobs and extra pounds and our children's books and our unstylish clothes.

We're trapped by our unrealistic dreams and by the inappropriate dreams of others. We're trapped by the fear of pursuing our possibilities. We're trapped by the pain of trying to achieve them and falling short.

But the pain isn't inevitable.

For years, I believed myself to be the most despicable being possible because my Church told me so. Yet when I came out and learned the history, science, and culture behind gay life, I no longer felt that anguish. It wasn't that I chose not to feel it anymore. The pain disappeared on its own once I realized its origin was entirely artificial.

I remember Lucy helping Ricky audition for his role as Don Juan. When she keeps hogging the audition so *she* can be discovered, she's tied to a bench to keep her in her place. And when she repeats her line, "Oh, that I could cut these ties that bind me!" she delivers it with real feeling.

Lucy Ricardo never makes it in Hollywood.

But we all love her anyway.

Perhaps we should begin to sing a love song to ourselves at least once a day. Make it our personal opening credit.

We've heard it a thousand times. "Be true to yourself." "Find your passion." "Dance like nobody's watching." The problem, of course, is that we only hear this counsel from "successful" people, which undercuts the message. Oprah found her passion, didn't she? So if I follow that advice…

No, we can't all be Oprah. And we shouldn't want to be. She does a great job of that by herself.

Let's do what *we* want to do with *our* lives. Hopefully, it's something that helps the world and doesn't hurt. But we can't *make* ourselves "be good" if it's not something we really want. On a note card taped to the top of my computer screen, I've written in bold letters, "Happiness isn't the goal. Lead a meaningful life." We must trust ourselves to make reasonably good decisions and be willing to adjust them as we go along. And if that doesn't bring us everything we ever wanted, that *has* to be OK.

Because "success" can never be anything more than making a handful of pivotal decisions in the course of an entire lifetime, whatever their outcome.

Let's make a good decision today.

Before Things Turned Violent

(published in *LA Progressive* on 3 June 2020)

I didn't want to go to the protest. Demonstrations in other cities the previous two evenings had grown violent. I couldn't even chop up an onion for dinner without wearing swim goggles. How would I get through being tear gassed? And this was Seattle, where a handful of anarchists had turned a peaceful protest at the WTO conference in 1999 into the Battle of Seattle. I'd moved here after that, but friends recounted coming home from work that evening and being beaten by police officers as they stepped off the bus, unaware till that moment that chaos reigned across half the city.

One of my favorite Osmond songs growing up was "One Bad Apple Don't Spoil the Whole Bunch, Girl," and maybe that was true. But it didn't take many more than that to ruin a protest.

It was 55 degrees this afternoon and raining lightly, the kind of weather that could calm a tense mood. "Please, please, please, God," I wanted to pray, "don't let agitators and accelerationists ruin everything." Too many white people across the country were looking for a reason to dismiss the protests. I could already see friends of mine online, liberals as well as conservatives, looking for an excuse not to care.

Gary and I parked on First Avenue near Pioneer Square at the southern end of downtown, a beautiful area but a little scary in the best of times. My husband was volunteering as security for his group of socialist friends, so we'd arrived forty minutes before the protest was to begin at 3:00. He headed off to walk the last fourteen blocks to Westlake while I stayed in the truck. A temporary assignment I'd been given through one of my part-time jobs had required me to remain on my feet the entire shift three days a week and I'd developed plantar fasciitis. I didn't want to aggravate the condition any more than necessary.

I'd lost my other part-time job when the pandemic started.

I was one of the lucky ones. My loss wasn't even part of the 40 million unemployment applications of the past two months.

Watching Gary walk off, I also saw homeless people who predated the financial crisis huddled in doorway after doorway. Every store was closed. No one needed to pass through those doors anymore, so folks practiced social distancing as best they could.

A young man across the street leaned against a building, drinking from a cup as he watched me for the next five minutes. And the next ten after that. He was *loitering.* As I was. But was he waiting for me to leave so he could vandalize the truck? Thieves had broken into Gary's pickup at least three times in the thirteen years we'd been together.

It was time for me to head to Westlake. I secured my face mask and started walking. A block up the street, I casually glanced back to see if anyone had approached the truck. No one had, so I continued on. Homeless folks had even set up tents where they could. A dozen men and women wrapped in sleeping bags and filthy jackets huddled under the glass pergola near the totem pole in front of the closed Underground Seattle, trying to stay dry.

"Please, God, help this protest be a force for good."

Seattle officials routinely ordered sweeps of the many homeless encampments throughout the city. Tents and all other belongings were confiscated and thrown away, as if that would somehow force the destitute to change their lives for the better.

I passed another man in a sleeping bag right in the middle of the sidewalk, one hand grasping the base of his roller suitcase as he slept.

Brian, one of my liberal friends, hated homeless people. "They're breaking the law!"

It's difficult not to break the law when poverty is criminalized.

But I was scared of "them," too. As I approached a mentally ill woman shouting obscenities at the universe, I debated on how best to pass by without enraging her even further. Walking too closely would certainly set her off, but creating too large a safety zone by walking in the middle of the street could easily be offensive and set her off as well.

I walked along the curb, avoiding eye contact. Not seeing her was offensive, too, of course. I wished I knew the right thing to do.

Passing a narrow alley, I got a whiff of ammonia, making me aware I was already starting to feel pressure in my bladder. I'd tried not to drink much after noon today, but my diabetes made it difficult to go more than two or three hours without a pee break. We'd left the house at 1:45, yet here it was not quite 3:00, and my bladder was already demanding attention.

More and more people were heading north now, most of them white, several carrying signs. "We stand with our black brothers and sisters." "Injustice anywhere is a threat to justice everywhere." "Remaining neutral in the face of injustice is to choose the side of the oppressor."

Back in middle school, a kid in my history class had bullied me repeatedly. When I told my mother, she urged me to hit him as hard as I could. But I didn't want to. It wasn't that I was afraid he'd hit me back even harder, though that was certainly a consideration. I simply didn't want to hurt anybody at all.

But I did say something snarky to the guy, and I remembered his eyes turning cold. "I'll see you out on the playground at lunch."

During lunch period, I remained in the hallway, avoiding both the cafeteria and the playground. But a teacher discovered me and, even after I explained the situation, ordered me out of the building. I could see the disgust in her eyes because I was afraid to face the bully.

The bully, naturally, spotted me within seconds and came over to start pushing me about. I think he may have hit me in the arm as well. But what I remember most from the confrontation was the older brother of a friend of mine walking over and telling the bully to leave me alone.

The bully walked away.

All these years later, I still preferred words to physical confrontation. But because of the pandemic, I didn't have a workplace to go to. Since I qualified as high risk, I'd had to opt for teleworking until my foot healed and I could return to a more normal assignment. Even now, favoring my left foot as much as possible, I could already feel the twinges that indicated possible new damage if I wasn't careful.

But I could hardly compare the risk of a small tear in one of my tendons to the danger blacks faced every time they stepped out of the house. I'd seen a Facebook post earlier from a man who said he never took a stroll around his mostly white neighborhood without walking his dog at the same time and asking his young daughter to accompany them. It was the only way he felt he could avoid being viewed as a criminal.

As a gay man, I understood the importance of allies. I might not be a *great* ally for Black Lives Matter, but I couldn't pretend I bore no obligation to help. The fact that I actually had a choice about participating today only proved my privilege once again.

I passed more and more police cars, officers in bulletproof vests on their bicycles, two EMT vehicles parked in anticipation. Dozens of people hurried past me on their way to Westlake. I walked slowly and carefully. Even the slight incline was making me puff.

Damn, this mask was *hot*. I could barely—

Hundreds of people packed the plaza in front of Westlake. I could hear the deep voice of a speaker, but the sound system seemed faulty. Though the words were loud enough, they were too muffled to understand. The protest signs, however, declared the message most of us were feeling. "We need an elected review board!" "Demilitarize the police!" "Silence is betrayal!"

I remembered the "Silence = Death" protest signs during the height of the AIDS crisis.

Two young white women in make-up that disguised their faces stopped me on the sidewalk. "Make sure you keep your mask on. They're using tear gas over there." One of the women pointed vaguely in the direction of the plaza.

No one was yelling. Protesters weren't running in fear. I saw no smoke, smelled nothing odd. Were these women just trying to keep people from joining the main crowd?

There were hundreds more people on the sidewalk near me and on the street separating us from the thickest part of the protest. Close enough for white complacency. I backed up against a storefront and tried to gauge the mood of those around me.

Everything seemed calm. This was already the second protest of the day, and nothing untoward had occurred during the first one as far as I knew. Thank god for Seattle rain.

"We can't sit in silence," one sign floating past me along the sidewalk declared. "Arrest complicit cops!" read another. "White people—show your work!" At least half of the people here were white.

How many, I wondered, were white supremacists? Gary had attended several counter-protests at Proud Boys rallies the past few years, always volunteering as security for his friends. The Pacific Northwest, I'd found to my dismay, was home to many white supremacist groups. Patriot Prayer had headquarters up here. A group of Three Percenters was in the area, too. I'd moved away from the south fifteen years ago, for God's sake. Things were supposed to be better here.

I couldn't see Gary anywhere in the crowd. If things got ugly…

I heard a rushing sound increasing in intensity. OMG, what was happening? Was that noise gas cannisters going off? I looked around quickly.

The crowd across the street was cheering something the speaker had just said.

Stop being such a scaredy-cat.

It was only 3:20, and I really had to pee. But another surprise like that, and I wouldn't need to worry about trying to find a bathroom.

The two white women near me kept stopping newcomers and warning them about the tear gas.

There was no tear gas.

Forty feet to my right, a black woman began yelling loudly at a white man. Everyone around them watched the altercation in silence. Finally, I heard the woman say, "We don't need any of you goddamn anarchists here! Get out!" After another minute of her outburst, the white man, clad all in black, walked off.

People turned their attention back to the speaker, clapping every once in a while. Apparently, others could make out the words I couldn't.

But did anyone believe that anarchist had simply gone home in defeat? And how many others were out there? Some days, I loathed people.

Some days, even myself.

A white man sitting on the sidewalk beside me handed out juice packets to homeless people who wandered by. Maybe they weren't even wandering. They seemed to know him, went right up to him. Maybe he did this all the time.

Another white man, barefaced, marched up to me in disgust. "Why are you wearing a mask? The pandemic's a hoax!" He walked away, shouting at other stupid people in the crowd. Most of us wore cloth masks, some wore paper masks, and a couple wore some version of gas mask. One man walked about in a snorkeling mask over his N95.

I patted my jacket pocket to make sure my swim goggles were ready if the warning from the two white women eventually turned out to be true.

Only 3:30, and Gary had told me the protest would probably last two hours. If I walked back to Pioneer Square, perhaps I could pee in an alley. It must happen there all the time.

A black man walked by, holding his sign up high. "I can't breathe!" Several of his friends followed behind as he moved on, each with a sign of his own.

"Listen!"

"Don't shoot! I'm asleep!"

"I can't believe we're still protesting this shit!"

Seattleites were all about recycling. I'd seen that last sign at another protest three or four years ago.

Three medics in PPE walked by with their gear, heading deeper into the crowd. Had something happened? Everyone still seemed calm.

A black woman in her late thirties moved up to an empty spot along the wall beside me. Her sign read, "PTSD—Present Traumatic Stress Disorder."

What the hell was wrong with so many white people? Why couldn't we just treat each other like human beings? Why were we so emotionally invested in refusing to demand change?

While perhaps 85% of the crowd was divided fairly equally between blacks and whites, a smaller but significant portion was composed of Asians and Latinx, with a few Native Americans and a smattering of other groups as well.

Damn, I needed to pee.

But I needed to stay at least till 4:00. A protest wasn't a place to just check in, say you were there, and head back out, marking off a box to prove you were "good." I needed to study more on how to be a better ally. Almost every form of oppression on the planet, after all, was tied either to racism or sexism.

Four young black men gathered along the wall several feet away, leaning in to talk like football players in a huddle. I was getting a bad vibe. They seemed suspicious.

Unless that was my subconscious bias popping up yet again.

This was all so hard. Not as hard as walking home with Skittles, of course, but still challenging. Was that why people wanted to wash their hands of it?

A young white man joined the two white women on my other side. The guy hooked something black to his belt. It was the shape of a soda can, but only half the length, and black. Was that a flash grenade? Or were they called flash bombs? Flash bangs?

With the growing political unrest in this country, it was clear I was going to need to learn some new words.

For now, I was going to use my diabetes as an excuse and start looking for a bathroom. Perhaps a Starbucks might be open farther from the demonstration. At about 3:50, I started heading south. Two blocks later, I glanced to my left and saw a huge crowd up on Fifth marching toward City Hall or King County jail. Or maybe police headquarters. The three buildings were all within a couple of blocks of each other.

Every store I passed was closed, even Starbucks. Several store owners had boarded up their windows. For all I knew, that had happened weeks ago when the city was first put under a stay-at-home order. This was the first time in two and a half months that I'd ventured more than a few blocks from home.

It was impossible to know how much of the tension in protests across the country this week was a result of the relentless police killings of unarmed blacks, how much was a product of the non-stop barrage of hateful rhetoric coming from the White House, and how much was simply a consequence of forced isolation coupled with increasing economic despair.

That morning, a good friend of mine had posted on FB her disgust with the riots. "Listen up, black people! This does nothing for your cause." And with that, she brushed off any need to care any longer about solving the root problems. If those bad, stupid black people were going to behave like animals, white people didn't need to concern themselves over something as minor as racism. Criminals got what they deserved.

I remembered my dad, a High Priest in our Mormon congregation, buying a CB radio back in the 1970s, so happy for its help in avoiding cops when we drove two hours to visit his parents in Mississippi. He could finally speed with impunity.

Our home in a white suburb of New Orleans was burglarized twice by white teenagers.

I'd watched on the news yesterday evening as a peaceful, unresisting black CNN reporter and his crew were arrested as they broadcast live from Minneapolis. I watched as a white reporter in Louisville and her crew were shot with pepper balls by officers aiming directly at them.

Whose cause did that further?

I passed a homeless woman in running shorts, shivering in the rain.

I had almost reached Pioneer Square again, but I didn't want to pee on the street. Gary had asked me not to ride public transportation during the pandemic, and I had no desire to, either, but Metro had begun blocking off seats on its buses to force people to keep a reasonable distance while riding. I was tired, my left foot hurt, my bladder was about to burst, and I just wanted to go home. So when a 7 Prentice pulled up to the bus stop, I stepped aboard and found an unblocked seat.

As we passed the light rail station in the International District, I could see another huge crowd heading north toward police headquarters.

The bus had hardly gone three blocks down Rainier Avenue when a police car with its siren blaring zoomed past us heading downtown, on *our* side of the street.

That couldn't be good. But I didn't want to text Gary. If anything bad was going on over there, I didn't want to distract him.

The bus was crowded, a white homeless man with filthy pants sitting on top of a "Seat Closed" sign across the aisle, another white man who looked down and out but perhaps not homeless sat next to me and talked to a black woman a seat behind us. Someone boarded with their dog. Another man carried two bags of groceries.

Some guy kept talking and talking and talking, apparently to no one. A few minutes later, I heard a black man address the talker. "We're gonna give you a pass because you're crazy," he said.

My phone rang, and I saw Gary's name on the screen. "Where are you?" he asked. I could barely hear him.

"I'm good," I told him. "I'm—"

He interrupted me with a question. I tried to hear him in all the noise around me and then he stopped talking in mid-sentence. I called him back, but there was no answer.

Fuck! If he was in trouble, I couldn't help him by calling.

Was this the day a neo-Nazi finally showed up with an assault weapon and mowed down thirty people? Neo-Nazis had been caught trying to blow up a gay bar on Capitol Hill several years earlier. And I knew the Boogaloo movement wanted to foment another civil war. In a world where the President of the United States could retweet, "The only good Democrat is a dead Democrat," anything was possible.

Damn, I needed to pee.

Finally, we reached my stop near the end of the line. I pulled the cord, the only thing I'd touched while aboard the bus. After we pulled to a stop, I stood up, avoiding the support bars, and headed to the door. I passed a black man asleep next to his belongings and stepped off.

The rain was pouring now. Thank God. Surely, that would slow down whatever was happening downtown.

I reached the house five minutes later, just a few minutes past 5:00. As soon as I unlocked the door, my phone vibrated and sent out a screech. "Emergency Alert!" The mayor had issued a curfew, effective at 5:00.

I ran to the bathroom and let out a long stream.

Remembering the hundreds of homeless people I'd seen that day who couldn't even use the bathroom in the public library anymore.

When I turned on the TV a moment later, I gasped. Cars were on fire downtown. Smoke from the promised tear gas was everywhere. A white man who might have grabbed a rifle from a vandalized police vehicle had the weapon ripped out of his hand by a white officer. People were breaking windows at Nordstrom and other stores, running inside and handing goods to people on the sidewalk.

Every one of the looters looked black.

Goddammit.

I'd seen a meme on FB earlier. "Looting isn't protesting. But murder isn't policing." Yet I knew almost all of my friends and family, both Republican and Democrat, were only going to remember the looting, not the murder of George Floyd or Breonna Taylor or anyone else. I knew my friends were also going to quibble over the term "murder" but would have no trouble lumping everyone at the protests with "thugs."

They'd already been saying for days that we shouldn't judge all cops by the bad behavior of a few bad officers. But they were already judging the entire Black Lives Matter movement by the actions of a minority of blacks destroying property.

On the TV in front of me, one of the news cameras zeroed in on several of the looters in the store. Over half of them were white. They were wearing ski masks that covered everything but their eyes and mouths. Black ski masks. But at least half of those looters were white. Not all of them. There were clearly some blacks looting as well.

And I knew most people across the country would only see black people committing crimes. The only time they bothered to notice black people at all.

And the looting and attacks on police cars might well have taken place without any prodding by white provocateurs. There was plenty of well-earned anger out there.

A reporter onscreen lamented that the protest had been going so well "before things turned violent." Did he *still* not understand the violence perpetrated against blacks for centuries?

I wondered if the black protesters I'd seen today wished I hadn't come down to Westlake at all. Had they been glad to see so many white faces, feeling they'd finally gained allies who'd stand with them when it counted, or had experience warned them to expect a hijacking?

Agents had infiltrated protests and strikes for the past 150 years, when women demanded suffrage, when blacks demanded suffrage, when workers demanded fair wages and safe working conditions. It was *always* going to happen, especially when the stakes were high.

But women did have the right to vote now. So did blacks. Workers did have unions.

So maybe as a society we'd finally make progress on this front, too, despite the sabotage.

The truth is we'll never be able to sift out who did what and which group they were part of. The best we can do is keep the focus on the source of the actual problem—structural racism that leads inevitably to individual racist atrocities.

I'd texted Gary the moment I turned on the television to let him know I'd made it home safely. He hadn't responded, hadn't answered when I called one more time. I kept my phone in front of me, glancing at it every fifteen seconds as if it were a rearview mirror.

Gary was a smart guy. He'd be home soon.

I remembered the twelve people huddled under the pergola in Pioneer Square.

The phone rang. Gary had made it back to the truck with two elderly women from his political group. I assured him I was fine, he assured me they were as well, and he told me he'd be home as soon as he could drop them off at their homes. "But, man, I really gotta pee."

I was waiting on the front porch when he drove up in the rain, holding the front door open as he ran past me to the bathroom.

About the Author

Johnny Townsend earned an MFA in fiction writing from Louisiana State University. He was also awarded a BA and MA in English, as well as a BS in Biology. A native of New Orleans, Townsend relocated to Seattle in the aftermath of Hurricane Katrina. After attending a Baptist high school for four years as a teenager, he volunteered as a Mormon missionary in Italy and then held positions in his local New Orleans ward as Second Councilor in the Elders Quorum, Ward Single Adult Representative, Stake Single Adult Chair, Sunday School Teacher, Stake Missionary, and Ward Membership Clerk. In the secular world, Townsend worked as a bookstore clerk, a college English instructor, a bank teller, a loan processor, a mail carrier, a library associate, a receptionist, and a professional escort. He worked selling bus passes, installing insulation, delivering pizza, cleaning residential construction sites, rehabilitating developmentally disabled adults, surveying gas stations, translating documents from Italian into English, preparing surgical carts for medical teams, and performing experiments on rat brains in a physiology lab.

Townsend has published stories and essays in *Newsday*, *The Washington Post*, *The Los Angeles Times*, *The Salt Lake Tribune*, *The Seattle Times*, *The Orlando Sentinel*, *The Army Times*, *The Humanist*, *The Progressive*, *Medical Reform*, *Christopher Street*, *The Massachusetts Review*, *Glimmer Train*, *Sunstone*, *Dialogue: A Journal of Mormon Thought*, in the anthologies *Queer Fish*, *Off the Rocks*, *Moth and Rust*, *The*

Kindness of Strangers, and *In Our Lovely Deseret: Mormon Fictions.* He helped edit *Latter-Gay Saints,* a collection of stories about gay Mormons, and he is the author of 43 books.

Most of those books are collections of Mormon short stories, of which several were named to Kirkus Reviews' Best of 2011, 2012, 2013, 2014, and 2015. In addition to his Mormon stories, Townsend has written a collection of Jewish stories, *The Golem of Rabbi Loew,* based on his years as a Jew. He has also written one non-fiction book, *Let the Faggots Burn: The UpStairs Lounge Fire,* having interviewed survivors as well as friends and relatives of the 32 people who were killed when an arsonist set fire to a gay bar in the French Quarter of New Orleans on Gay Pride Day in 1973. He is an Associate Producer of the feature-length documentary *Upstairs Inferno,* directed by Robert Camina.

Townsend sang in the New Orleans Gay Men's Chorus for a time and performed in the priests' chorus in the opera *Aida.* He has a collection of Victorian ceramic tiles, wooden dinosaur carvings from Bali, and the entire set of Calvin and Hobbes comic strip compilations in Italian. In addition to speaking English and Italian, he's also studied French, Spanish, Russian, Hebrew, Old English, and American Sign Language. Townsend is an avid movie fan, whose three favorite Hitchcock films are *Shadow of a Doubt,* *Strangers on a Train,* and *Rear Window.* He gives regularly to environmental conservation groups, medical charities, groups that support single-payer healthcare, human rights organizations, and to various documentaries and other projects he finds on crowdfunding sites.

The University of Utah in Salt Lake City has a Special Collection of Townsend material, including all his books, the magazines and newspapers that have published his work, his journals, his correspondence, photographs, and even a portrait painted by a prominent gay artist. ONE Archives in Los Angeles, the national LGBTQ archive, has his UpStairs Lounge materials and his 20 original gay quilts.

Johnny Townsend is married to Gary Tolman, another former Mormon who worked in the same mission in Italy. They still speak Italian to each other regularly.

Books by Johnny Townsend

Thanks for reading! If you enjoyed this book, could you please take a few minutes to write a review online? Reviews are helpful both to me as an author and to other readers, so we'd all sincerely appreciate your writing one! And if you did enjoy the book, here are some others I've written you might want to look up:

Mormon Underwear

God's Gargoyles

The Circumcision of God

Sex among the Saints

Dinosaur Perversions

Zombies for Jesus

The Abominable Gayman

The Gay Mormon Quilter's Club

The Golem of Rabbi Loew

Mormon Fairy Tales

Flying over Babel

Marginal Mormons

Mormon Bullies

The Mormon Victorian Society

Dragons of the Book of Mormon

Selling the City of Enoch

A Day at the Temple

Behind the Zion Curtain

Gayrabian Nights

Lying for the Lord

Despots of Deseret

Missionaries Make the Best Companions

Invasion of the Spirit Snatchers

The Tyranny of Silence

Sex on the Sabbath

The Washing of Brains

The Mormon Inquisition

Interview with a Mission President

Weeping, Wailing, and Gnashing of Teeth

Behind the Bishop's Door

The Moat around Zion

The Last Days Linger

Mormon Madness

Human Compassion for Beginners

Dead Mankind Walking

Who Invited You to the Orgy?

Breaking the Promise of the Promised Land

I Will, Through the Veil

Am I My Planet's Keeper?

Have Your Cum and Eat It, Too

Strangers with Benefits

What Would Anne Frank Do?

Let the Faggots Burn: The UpStairs Lounge Fire

Latter-Gay Saints: An Anthology of Gay Mormon Fiction (co-editor)

Available from BookLocker.com or your favorite online or neighborhood bookstore.

Wondering what some of those other books are about? Read on!

The Washing of Brains

A world-weary man becomes a widower for the third time. A man awakens to celebrate a milestone birthday only to discover that horrifying world events demand his attention instead. A budding feminist tries to make a political statement by giving birth to her "illegitimate" son in church just before Mother's Day. Missionaries in Rome try to prevent a terrorist bombing. The Prophet devises a plan to reverse global warming. A Salt Lake bishop is overwhelmed by his congregants' secrets. A gay Mormon man devastated by the breakup of his marriage to a closeted Hasidic Jew considers returning to the fold. An unhappy bartender reminisces about the affair he had with his mission president in Paris. A returned missionary takes a job in an adult video store. A young woman befriends the dungeon master who lives above her. A BYU student working as an escort finds love.

Invasion of the Spirit Snatchers

During the Apocalypse, a group of Mormon survivors in Hurricane, Utah gather in the home of the Relief Society president, telling stories to pass the time as they ration their food storage and await the Second Coming. But this is no ordinary group of Mormons—or perhaps it is. They are the faithful, feminist, gay, apostate, and repentant, all working together to help each other through the darkest days any of them have yet seen.

Gayrabian Nights

Gayrabian Nights is a twist on the well-known classic, *1001 Arabian Nights*, in which Scheherazade, under the threat of death if she ceases to captivate King Shahryar's attention, enchants him through a series of mysterious, adventurous, and romantic tales.

In this variation, a male escort, invited to the hotel room of a closeted, homophobic Mormon senator, learns that the man is poised to vote on a piece of anti-gay legislation the following morning. To prevent him from sleeping, so that the exhausted senator will miss casting his vote on the Senate floor, the escort entertains him with stories of homophobia, celibacy, mixed orientation marriages, reparative therapy, coming out, first love, gay marriage, and long-term successful gay relationships. The escort crafts the stories to give the senator a crash course in gay culture and sensibilities, hoping to bring the man closer to accepting his own sexual orientation.

Let the Faggots Burn: The UpStairs Lounge Fire

On Gay Pride Day in 1973, someone set the entrance to a French Quarter gay bar on fire. In the terrible inferno that followed, thirty-two people lost their lives, including a third of the local congregation of the Metropolitan Community Church, their pastor burning to death halfway out a second-story window as he tried to claw his way to freedom. A mother who'd gone to the bar with her two gay sons died alongside them. A man who'd helped his friend escape first was found dead near the fire escape. Two children waited outside a movie theater across town for a father and step-father who would never pick them up. During this era of rampant homophobia, several families refused to claim the bodies, and many churches refused to bury the dead. Author Johnny Townsend pored through old records and tracked down survivors of the fire as well as relatives and friends of those killed to compile this fascinating account of a forgotten moment in gay history.

The Abominable Gayman

What is a gay Mormon missionary doing in Italy? He is trying to save his own soul as well as the souls of others. In these tales chronicling the two-year mission of Robert Anderson, we see a young man tormented by his inability to be the man the Church says he should be. In addition to his personal hell, Anderson faces a major earthquake, organized crime, a serious bus accident, and much more. He copes with horrendous mission leaders and his own suicidal tendencies. But one day, he meets another missionary who loves him, and his world changes forever.

Marginal Mormons

What happens when a High Priest becomes addicted to crack cocaine? Do gay people have positive near-death experiences or unhappy ones? Is there a way to splice the empathy gene into the genome of every human? Can a schizophrenic woman on anti-delusional drugs still keep her belief in an intangible God? Will a childless biochemist be able to find fulfillment by taking part in a mission to Mars? Not every Latter-day Saint has a mainstream story to tell, but these soul-searching people are still more than the marginal Mormons headquarters would like us to believe.

Despots of Deseret

In this collection of Mormon short stories, a man learns to forgive his mother for an unspeakable atrocity. An uncle awaits word on his niece caught up in the 2004 tsunami. A bereaved man receives an unexpected gift from his deceased husband on Valentine's Day. A stake president threatens to revoke a couple's temple marriage. A young woman faces a shocking tragedy while serving as a missionary in Paraguay. A Mormon teenager wants to be named Best Christian Example at his Baptist high school. An anti-Mormon mob threatens a church outing. A virginal gay man takes out a contract on his own life to protect his virtue.

Sex among the Saints

Clean-cut Mormons may preach purity and wholesomeness, but sometimes repressing sexual instincts forces those feelings to erupt in unexpected ways. Here, two young women vie for the sexual affections of the same missionary. An elderly farmer marries his best friend's mistress in order to feel closer to both of them. A woman is dumped by the husband who gave her HIV. A woman fantasizes about her sex life as one of Jesus' future wives. These tales are not for those who deny the reality of sexuality, but the rest of us will enjoy getting a glimpse into the Mormon bedroom.

Missionaries Make the Best Companions

What lies behind the freshly scrubbed façades of the Mormon missionaries we see about town? In these stories, an ex-Mormon tries to seduce a faithful elder by showing him increasingly suggestive movies. A sister missionary fulfills her community service requirement by babysitting for a prostitute. Two elders break their mission rules by venturing into the forbidden French Quarter. A senior missionary couple try to reactivate lapsed members while their own family falls apart back home. A young man hopes that serving a second full-time mission will lead him up the Church hierarchy. Two bored missionaries decide to make a little extra money moonlighting in a male stripper club. Two frustrated elders find an acceptable way to masturbate—by donating to a Fertility Clinic. A lonely man searches for the favorite companion he hasn't seen in thirty years.

Dragons of the Book of Mormon

A supporter of Prop 8 is forced to attend his boss's gay wedding. A devout Latter-day Saint struggling to pay his bills wonders if he should keep paying tithing, even after being excommunicated. A reporter seeks the identity of Salt Lake's new superhero—a masked man wearing temple clothes who mysteriously shows up at crime scenes. A woman is murdered in the temple on her wedding day. One of the Three Nephites is missing in Pasadena. Mormons survive the zombie apocalypse because of their two-year supply of food storage.

Mormon Underwear

Mormon Underwear tells the stories of gay Mormons that mainstream members don't want to hear. Whether it is a young LDS man stripping to his Mormon underwear in public or a virginal 70-year-old finally giving in to temptation, a straight son who discovers his father kissing another man or a group who plots to put gays into positions of power within the Church, these are the stories too shameful or shocking to be told among traditional Saints.

The Golem of Rabbi Loew

Jacob and Esau Cohen are the closest of brothers. In fact, they're lovers. A doctor tries to combine canine genes with those of Jews, to improve their chances of surviving a hostile world. A Talmudic scholar dates an escort. A scientist tries to develop the "God spot" in the brains of his patients in order to create a messiah. The Golem of Prague is really Rabbi Loew's secret lover. While some of the Jews in Townsend's book are Orthodox, this collection of Jewish stories most certainly is not.

God's Gargoyles

These tales of gay Mormons reveal abominable yet delightful secrets. A gay couple steals from the rich to provide for their favorite charities. A celibate 38-year-old dates a promiscuous porn reviewer. A schizophrenic man accustomed to hearing voices suddenly starts to receive real revelations.

Mormon Fairy Tales

In these stories, we discover how the Three Nephites from the Book of Mormon cope with their frustrated sexuality when their wives aren't immortal as they are. A deceased sinner plots to break out of Spirit Prison. A polygamist in 1855 Utah is ordered to take a fourth wife, when all he really wants is to be with another man. A disappointed wife plots revenge when her temple worker husband sues the Church for an on-the-job injury. Aliens visiting the UN reveal that God really does live on a planet orbiting Kolob.

The Mormon Victorian Society

A Victorian enthusiast has a startling sexual revelation to make at his monthly Society meeting. Two men find love in the aftermath of Hurricane Katrina. A home teaching assignment goes terribly wrong when a man whose father was murdered in a gay bar is confronted with a young gay cowboy. A Relief Society president is trapped on a plane next to a gay man flaunting his sexuality. A ministering angel to a young god tires of his position. Gay Mormons react when the Prophet has a new revelation about homosexuality.

Lying for the Lord

In this collection of Mormon short stories, a missionary in Italy makes a break for freedom on Christmas. A youth outing for priests at a shooting range doesn't go as planned. Mormons create a theocracy in America and rename the country Zion. A conflicted father wonders how to deal with a transgender daughter. A bishop devises a novel method to make sure his congregants pass Tithing Settlement. Parents hire men to pose as the Three Nephites to teach their children the Book of Mormon is true. Ex-Mormons unwelcome at home for Christmas band together for their own holiday celebration.

Sex on the Sabbath

A missionary in Italy tries to rescue a woman enslaved in trafficking. A Salt Lake bishop is murdered in his office. A Mormon advice columnist gets into trouble with the Church. Parents arrange to kidnap their missionary son and force him into deprogramming. A disabled woman questions her Patriarchal Blessing's admonition to remain celibate her entire life. A husband chafes when his wife won't let him watch R-rated movies. A straight high school senior asks his gay friend to the prom. Even a near-death experience doesn't convince a skeptic of the existence of God. A chaste Single Adult group ventures into the French Quarter on Mardi Gras.

The Tyranny of Silence

An Artificial Intelligence tries to lead Mormons astray. The Church addresses the perils of inappropriate hair styles for men. A bereaved widow listens to the radio hoping to hear love songs from her departed husband. A prankster makes life miserable for his LDS boss. An ex-Mormon earns a living selling Mormon underwear online to non-members. A young man fakes a two-year mission to please his family. Another missionary targets potential converts on dating sites. A lonely husband pays the price for straying from his wife. The Church reels after a leak that children of gay couples can no longer participate in its saving rituals and ordinances. A depressed Santa reaches out to help his community.

Selling the City of Enoch

In this collection of Mormon short stories, we see a mission president's wife murdered in Rome. An abused man learns to love for the first time. A mother plans for her role as a god in the hereafter. A descendant of Enoch tries out capitalism. A bishop disguises himself as a homeless man to teach his congregation a lesson. A lonely young woman rents a mother and father for Christmas. A young husband is horrified to learn he has married a pre-op male-to-female trans woman in the temple. A group of ex-Mormons meet regularly to watch LDS movies in order to keep in touch with their culture.

The Last Days Linger

The scriptures tell us that in the Last Days, wickedness will increase upon the Earth. When leaders of the Mormon Church see a rise in the number of gay members, they believe the end is upon them. But while "wickedness never was happiness," it begins to appear that wickedness can sometimes be divine. At least, the stories here suggest that religious proscriptions condemning homosexuality have it all wrong. While gay Mormons may be no closer to perfection than anyone else, they're no further from it, either. And sometimes, being gay provides just the right ingredient to create saints—as flawed as God himself.

The Moat around Zion

A moat can work to keep bad guys out of one's sanctuary, but it can also act like a prison, trapping good people inside, and the stench from its fetid waters can often prove unbearable. In these tales of the trapped faithful, a woman is shunned when a hacker fakes her apostasy from the Mormon Church. A young missionary can't get permission to see a doctor about the lump on his testicle until he can convince his mission president he isn't masturbating. A lesbian couple wonder if their desperate financial situation is a punishment from God. A teenage girl impersonates her brother so she can perform baptisms for the dead in the temple. Two gay missionaries in Italy fall in love.

Mormon Madness

Mental illness can strike the faithful as easily as anyone else. But often religious doctrine and practice exacerbate rather than alleviate these problems. From schizophrenia to obsessive-compulsive disorder, from persecution complex to sexual dysfunction, autism to dissociative identity disorder, Mormons must cope with their mental as well as their spiritual health on a daily basis.

Human Compassion for Beginners

The battle to direct legislation and policy often seems to be a fight between greed and compassion. Emotions run so high that family members stop speaking to one another and long-time friendships fall by the wayside. But the problems being debated—climate change, universal healthcare, LGBTQ rights, gun regulation, economic inequality, and the separation of church and state—desperately need to be resolved.

Dead Mankind Walking

Do you yell at the TV while watching the news? Do you repost maddening articles on Facebook? Do you find yourself overwhelmed by the 200 new political emails in your inbox every day? Left, right, center, far left, or far right, we can't escape the political battles of our time.

What this collection of essays and op-eds from *LA Progressive*, *The Salt Lake Tribune*, and *Main Street Plaza* can do is help us understand and address many of the concerns that affect almost every aspect of our lives: structural racism, gerrymandering, voting rights, regressive taxes, political infighting, the failure of capitalism, and the ever present overstep of religion in public policy.

But of all the issues covered here, the most urgent is climate change. If we can't address that one, the others don't much matter, since every one of us all too soon becomes nothing more than a tiny, inescapable part of *Dead Mankind Walking.*

Breaking the Promise of the Promised Land: How Religious Conservatives Failed America

By aligning themselves over the past 60 years with the most conservative wing of the Republican Party, Mormons became leading contributors to the cultural and moral decay of America. Mormon prophets have long declared that God set America apart for the righteous. It was to be a land of freedom, justice, and peace, a place where the Lamanites could blossom as the rose, a country so righteous that the affairs of the entire world would be conducted here during the Millennium.

But when Mormons tired of being "a peculiar people" and chose to side with the most repressive evangelicals, they chose to make America the land of the imprisoned, poor, and oppressed. While declaring their allegiance to the Prince of Peace, they've chosen to support policies that have kept America at war almost non-stop for the last six decades.

Am I My Planet's Keeper?

Global Warming. Climate Change. Climate Crisis. Climate Emergency. Whatever label we use, we are facing one of the greatest challenges to the survival of life as we know it.

But while addressing greenhouse gases is perhaps our most urgent need, it's not our only task. We must also address toxic waste, pollution, habitat destruction, and our other contributions to the world's sixth mass extinction event.

In order to do that, we must simultaneously address the unmet human needs that keep us distracted from deeper engagement in stabilizing our climate: moderating economic inequality, guaranteeing healthcare to all, and ensuring education for everyone.

And to accomplish *that*, we must unite to combat the monied forces that use fear, prejudice, and misinformation to manipulate us.

It's a daunting task. But success is our only option.

I Will, Through the Veil

What gay man hasn't fantasized about hot sex with those repressed Mormon missionaries in their white shirts and conservative ties? But there's more to Mormon fantasy sex than curious young "elders." What about temple workers going at it in the baptismal font after hours? How about an ex-Mormon who throws a "pity party" (or "pity orgy") for men whose physical flaws prevent them from getting laid regularly? The ex-mo trapped by a snowstorm in an adult video store overnight? Or the one who offers "aid" to detectives investigating a shooting? And what collection of gay Mormon porn would be complete without an adventure involving the sexual practices the Three Nephites have perfected over two thousand years?

Have Your Cum and Eat It, Too

It's 1981, and two Mormon missionaries randomly assigned to work together as "companions" in Napoli find themselves in trouble. They're falling in love, but the Church forbids gay relationships. As missionaries, they can't date anyone at all, much less other men. If they're found out, they'll be excommunicated, sent home in disgrace, and cast out from their families.

In the aftermath of a devastating earthquake, against a backdrop of poverty and repressive mission culture, Elders Grant and Mortensen knock on doors, endure violent assaults, and face the ultimate challenge—will they be crushed by dedication to their beliefs or will love provide a way for them to escape?

Strangers with Benefits

Two Mormon missionaries knocking on doors in New Orleans come upon a gay couple who help them unleash their repressed sexuality, leading them to begin a clandestine love affair carried out in the back rooms of gay bars and French Quarter bathhouses.

Knowing that excommunication means abandonment by family and friends, they race to save money by posing nude and dancing in stripper bars before they are discovered. Still intent on "serving" as missionaries, they take up escorting to give others their all.

But when disaster strikes, they must resolve their most challenging crisis of faith yet—can they be true to each other while leading a life of sexual service to their fellow man?

What Would Anne Frank Do?

In a world already plagued by the effects of late-stage capitalism—economic inequality, voter suppression, healthcare inequality, racial injustice, and an escalating climate crisis—how do we continue fighting for meaningful progress in the middle of a pandemic?

These essays and op-eds from the *Salt Lake Tribune*, the *Seattle Times*, and *LA Progressive* show us that unity can be divisive, morality can be immoral, and facts can be fabricated. But no one ever said fighting against manipulation and willful ignorance was easy.

In this collection, author Johnny Townsend offers encouragement and insight gained from his own experience as a climate crisis refugee and human rights activist.

Publications

Books

What Would Anne Frank Do? BookLocker.com, June 2020

Strangers with Benefits, BookLocker.com, May 2020

Am I My Planet's Keeper? BookLocker.com, Feb 2020

Have Your Cum and Eat It, Too, BookLocker.com, Jan 2020

I Will, Through the Veil, BookLocker.com, Oct 2019

Breaking the Promise of the Promised Land, BookLocker.com, Sept 2019

Who Invited You to the Orgy? BookLocker.com, June 2019

Dead Mankind Walking, BookLocker.com, Feb 2019

Human Compassion for Beginners, BookLocker.com, November 2018

Mormon Madness, BookLocker.com, June 2018

The Moat Around Zion, BookLocker.com, June 2018

The Last Days Linger, BookLocker.com, September 2017

Behind the Bishop's Door, BookLocker.com, July 2017

Weeping, Wailing, and Gnashing of Teeth, BookLocker.com, April 2017

Interview with a Mission President, BookLocker.com, January 2017

The Mormon Inquisition, BookLocker.com, October 2016

The Washing of Brains, BookLocker.com, August 2016

Sex on the Sabbath, BookLocker.com, April 2016

The Tyranny of Silence, BookLocker.com, January 2016

Invasion of the Spirit Snatchers, BookLocker.com, January 2016

Missionaries Make the Best Companions, BookLocker.com, August 2015

Despots of Deseret, BookLocker.com, April 2015

Lying for the Lord, BookLocker.com, February 2015

Gayrabian Nights, BookLocker.com, November 2014

Behind the Zion Curtain, BookLocker.com, November 2014

A Day at the Temple, BookLocker.com, July 2014

Selling the City of Enoch, BookLocker.com, March 2014

Dragons of the Book of Mormon, BookLocker.com, October 2013

The Mormon Victorian Society, BookLocker.com, March 2013

Mormon Bullies, BookLocker.com, July 2012

Marginal Mormons, BookLocker.com, July 2012

Flying over Babel, BookLocker.com, Jan 2012

Let the Faggots Burn: The UpStairs Lounge Fire, BookLocker.com, Aug 2011

Mormon Fairy Tales, BookLocker.com, Jan 2011

The Golem of Rabbi Loew, BookLocker.com, Aug 2010

The Gay Mormon Quilter's Club, BookLocker.com, Jun 2010

The Abominable Gayman, BookLocker.com, Feb 2010

Zombies for Jesus, BookLocker.com, Jan 2010

Dinosaur Perversions, BookLocker.com, Dec 2009

Sex among the Saints, BookLocker.com, Dec 2009

The Circumcision of God, BookLocker.com, Dec 2009

God's Gargoyles, BookLocker.com, Dec 2009

Mormon Underwear, BookLocker.com, Nov 2009

Books Edited

Latter-Gay Saints, edited by Gerald S. Argetsinger, Jeff Laver, and Johnny Townsend. Lethe Press, 2013.

Film

Upstairs Inferno, produced and directed by Robert Camina, Camina Entertainment. Associate Producer Johnny Townsend. 2015.

Essays

"Politics as Religious Conviction," published in *Main Street Plaza* on June 7, 2020

"Does Anybody Here Know How to Fly a Plane?" published in *LA Progressive* on June 7, 2020

"Things to Say to Police While Being Murdered," published in *LA Progressive* on June 3, 2020

"Before Things Turned Violent," published in *LA Progressive* on June 3, 2020

"Ban All Routine Traffic Stops," published in *LA Progressive* on May 30, 2020

"COVID Blankets for Poor People," published in *LA Progressive* on May 26, 2020

"The Religious Right and Right-Wing Death Panels," published by *LA Progressive* on May 25, 2020

"Securing the Well-Being of Citizens is not Tyranny," published in the *Salt Lake Tribune* on May 23, 2020

"The Democratic Party Can't Be Changed from Within," published in *LA Progressive* on May 21, 2020

"Give a Man a Check…" published in *LA Progressive* on May 18, 2020

"Consistent Messaging in an Emergency," published in *LA Progressive* on May 18, 2020

"Please Contact Me When You Have a Platform Worth Supporting," published in *LA Progressive* on May 12, 2020

"Zero is Not an Increment," published in *LA Progressive* on May 11, 2020

"Who Said It Best—Republicans or Democrats?" published in *LA Progressive* on May 6, 2020

"We Can't Eliminate Our Impact on Climate, But We Can Lessen It," published in *LA Progressive* on May 3, 2020

"Do Extremists Just Want to Kill People They Don't Like?" published in *LA Progressive* on April 29, 2020

"Progressives Must Accept It's OK to be Hated," published in *LA Progressive* on April 25, 2020

"LDS Church Should Send Its Members on Renewable Energy Missions," published in the *Salt Lake Tribune* on April 24, 2020

"Lotteries Are Essential…but They Shouldn't Be," published in *LA Progressive* on April 22, 2020

"Do We Really *Need* It or Do We Just Want It?" published in *LA Progressive* on April 15, 2020

"Republicans Need to Take Responsibility for Their Actions…and So Do Democrats," published in *LA Progressive* on April 12, 2020

"Which Scrooge Are You?" published in *LA Progressive* on April 4, 2020

"Democratic Voters Have a New Level of Expectation," published in *LA Progressive* on March 29, 2020

"My HIV Infection Taught Me to Treat Everyone as if They're Contagious," published in *LA Progressive* on March 26, 2020

"The LDS Church Should Create Solar and Wind Farms," published in the *Salt Lake Tribune* on March 21, 2020

"Borrowed Emergency," published in *LA Progressive* on March 8, 2020

"COVID-19 Isn't My First Pandemic," published in the *Seattle Times* on March 6, 2020

"The Gospel of Misery," published in *Main Street Plaza* on February 23, 2020

"Let's Stop Digging Our Own Graves," published in the *Salt Lake Tribune* on February 21, 2020

"It's Risky to Nominate a Democratic Socialist: It's Also Risky Not To," published in *LA Progressive* on February 14, 2020

"The Power of Positive Giving Up," published in the *Salt Lake Tribune* on January 19, 2020

"How I Learned to Promote My Own Books by Getting Paid to Promote Someone Else's," published in *Writers Weekly* on January 3, 2020

"The Answer to Climate Denial Can Be Found in Porn," published in *LA Progressive* on December 30, 2019

"Mormons Must Divest from Fossil Fuels," published in the *Salt Lake Tribune* on December 15, 2019

"That Time King Noah Had Our Back," published in *Main Street Plaza* on November 25, 2019

"The LDS Church Should Pay Off the Medical Debt of Its Members," published in the *Salt Lake Tribune* on November 2, 2019

"A Stingy God," published in *Main Street Plaza* on October 29, 2019

"Make Earth Great Again," published in *LA Progressive* on September 21, 2019

"Let's All Start Wearing Shorts to Church!" published in the *Salt Lake Tribune* on September 15, 2019

"Does the Second Anointing Explain Mormon Support for Trump?" published in *Main Street Plaza* on August 23, 2019

"Give Me Your Tired, Your Poor, Your Europeans," published in *LA Progressive* on August 15, 2019

"Climate Crisis Threatens the Mormon Church," published in *Main Street Plaza* on August 12, 2019

"'Realism' Is What Got Us into This Mess in the First Place," published in *LA Progressive* on August 3, 2019

"Woe unto Them That Are with Child," published in *Main Street Plaza* on August 3, 2019

"A War on Religion," published in *Main Street Plaza* on July 22, 2019

"My Mother's Forced Abortion and Sterilization," published in *LA Progressive* on July 13, 2019

"If Climate Change Is Real but Not Caused by Human Activity, Don't We Still Need to Address It?" published in the *Salt Lake Tribune* on June 23, 2019

"Don't Feed the Humans: Criminalizing Compassion," published in the *Orlando Sentinel* on June 18, 2019

"4 Out of 5 Oligarchs Give Up Their Money and Power When Asked Politely," published in *LA Progressive* on June 12, 2019

"With Friends Like These: The Liberal Media's Attack on Progressive Policies," published in *LA Progressive* on June 9, 2019

"Öl macht frei," published in *LA Progressive* on May 27, 2019

"Payday Loans Suck Life from the Poor," published in *LA Progressive* on May 20, 2019

"Eyes in the Back of My Head," published in *Main Street Plaza* on May 19, 2019

"When Protesting Genocide Is a Racist Act," published in the *Salt Lake Tribune* on May 12, 2019

"Chicken Little: One if by Land, Two if by Sea," published in *LA Progressive* on May 5, 2019

"Have I Been Wrong All This Time?" published in *LA Progressive* on April 24, 2019

"Superstition Is Leading Us Toward Extinction," published in the *Salt Lake Tribune* on April 21, 2019

"Democrats Must Change Their Mascot from the Donkey to the Ostrich," published in *LA Progressive* on April 17, 2019

"Bracing Ourselves for Climate Combat," published in the *Salt Lake Tribune* on March 24, 2019

"A Mormon By Any Other Name," published in *Main Street Plaza* on March 17, 2019

"Progressive Reform vs. Socialist Revolution," published in *LA Progressive* on March 8, 2019

"Pledging Allegiance to the DNC," published in *LA Progressive* on Feb 28, 2019

"I'm Two Days Older Than You, So I'm Always Right," published in *LA Progressive* on Feb 25, 2019

"Fearmongering on the Left," published in *LA Progressive* on Feb 21, 2019

"Parable of the Three Firefighters," published in *LA Progressive* on Feb 4, 2019

"Very Tiny Acts of Relative Kindness," published in *LA Progressive* on Feb 2, 2019

"Gerrymandered Out of Church," published in *Main Street Plaza* on Jan 17, 2019

"I Am Liberal, Hear Me Roar," published in *LA Progressive* on Jan 15, 2019

"Democrats Must Adapt to Political Climate Change...Or Go Extinct," published in *LA Progressive* on Jan 9, 2019

"I'm a Jew Who Wants to Boycott Israel," published in *LA Progressive* on Jan 5, 2019

"Blame Me for Losing or Do What It Takes to Win," published in *LA Progressive* on Jan 2, 2019

"Fossil Fuels Anonymous," published in *LA Progressive* on Jan 1, 2019

"Crazy Lady on the Bus," published in *LA Progressive* on Dec 30, 2018

"Our Nazi Who Art in Heaven," published in the *Salt Lake Tribune* on Dec 23, 2018

"Willing, Not Happy, To Pay Regressive Taxes," published in *LA Progressive* on Dec 11, 2018

"How Do We 'Demand' Justice?" published in *LA Progressive* on Nov 25, 2018

"Churches Must Encourage Their Members to Have Fewer Children," published in the *Salt Lake Tribune* on Nov 25, 2018

"Mandatory Courses on Race, Gender, and Social Justice," published in *LA Progressive* on Nov 23, 2018

"I'm Ashamed to Call Myself a Mormon," published in the *Salt Lake Tribune* on Oct 21, 2018

"Teetotalers for Legal Marijuana," published in the *Salt Lake Tribune* on Sept 11, 2018

"Moral Tyranny," published in *Main Street Plaza* on August 23, 2018

"Silence Isn't Deafening," published in *LA Progressive* on August 17, 2018

"Inasmuch As Ye Have Done It Unto One of the Least of These My Brethren, It Matters Not to Me," published in *Main Street Plaza* on August 13, 2018

"Mormons Hate Socialism, But Only in the United States," published in the *Salt Lake Tribune* on August 12, 2018

"Treating a Critically Ill Climate," published in *LA Progressive* on August 4, 2018

"Trump is Worse than AIDS," published in *LA Progressive* on July 30, 2018

"Shunning as Political Strategy," published in *LA Progressive* on July 28, 2018

"Protest Votes, Capitulation, or Vision?" published in *LA Progressive* on July 27, 2018

"Political Pragmatism Isn't Smart," published in *LA Progressive* on July 25, 2018

"I Will Not Live to Be 230 Years Old," published in *LA Progressive* on July 22, 2018

"My Reply to Fundraising Emails from Moderate Democrats," published in *LA Progressive* on July 15, 2018

"Appealing to Moderate Republicans Is Not the Answer," published in *LA Progressive* on July 2, 2018

"Porn Is Not a Public Health Crisis," published in the *Salt Lake Tribune*, Mar 4, 2018

"Become a Paid Expert by Writing Op-Eds," published in *Funds for Writers*, Nov 6, 2017

"Writing an Effective Author Bio," published in *Writers Weekly*, August 24, 2017

"Scott Abbott, *Immortal for Quite Some Time*," (review), *Western American Literature*, U of Nebraska, Vol. 52, No. 4, Winter 2018

"LGBTQ Lit for Mormons," published in the *Salt Lake Tribune*, July 2, 2017

"Submitting to Anthologies," published in *Writers Weekly*, June 22, 2017

"Drinking 7-Up on Bourbon Street," published in *Happy Hours—Our Lives in the Gay Bars*, eds. S. Renee Bess and Lee Lynch, Flashpoint Publications: Nov 2017

"Drowning in Belief," published in *Moth and Rust: Mormon Encounters with Death*, ed. Stephen Carter, Signature Books: Salt Lake, October 2017

"Gay Mormon Escort," published in *My Gay New Orleans*, ed. Frank Perez, LL Publications: Bedford, TX, July 2016.

"Striving for Excellence," published by *Kirkus Reviews*, June 30, 2016

"Will We Learn from Orlando? We Didn't Learn from New Orleans," published in the *Salt Lake Tribune* on June 19, 2016

"To Niche or Not to Niche," published by *Funds for Writers* on Feb 12, 2016

"The Senility of the Republican Party," published in *LA Progressive* on Dec 30, 2012

"Nukes Don't Kill People, People Kill People," published in *LA Progressive* on Dec 19, 2012

"An Air Freshener for the Outhouse," published in *LA Progressive* on Dec 18, 2012

"Gay Mormons Tie the Knot," published in *Religion Dispatches* on Nov 20, 2012

"The Abominable Gayman," book review published in the Autumn 2012 issue of *American Athenaeum*

"Why I Am Not a Traitor," published in the *Q Review*, Sept 2011

"Freshman Biology for Mormon Leaders," published in the *Q Review*, Dec 2010

"Environmental Serial Killers," published in *LA Progressive* on May 15, 2010

"Murderers of Old Men," published in *LA Progressive* on May 10, 2010

"All-American Degeneracy," published in the July 1997 issue (Vol. 57, #4) of *The Humanist*

"A Shot in the Arm," published in the November 1995 issue (Vol. 55, #6) of *The Humanist,* and in *Critical Thinking and Critical Reading*, by Pearson Custom Publishing (2009), a custom edition for Rio Salado College

"Student and Victim of Health Reform," published in the July 1995 issue of *The Free Press*

"A Father-Son Outing," published in the June 1995 issue (#12) of *A New Direction*

"The Eugenics of Health Care," published in the April 1995 issue (Vol. 15, #1) of *Medical Reform*

"The Virgin Prostitute," published in the Spring 1995 issue (Vol. 9, #1) of *Flipside*

"Gay Genes," published in the Spring 1995 issue (Vol. 4, #1) of *Gray Areas*

"Scholarships for Homophobia," published in the February 1995 issue of *The Free Press*

"Legal Marriage for Gay Hindus," published in issue #30 (1995) of the *LGLC Newsletter* (Libertarians for Gay and Lesbian Concerns)

"Criticism—the Defender of Insecurity," published in the April 1995 issue (#11) of *A New Direction*

"A Letter in Response to a Friend," published in the February 1995 issue (#10) of *A New Direction*

"God's Justice System," published in the February 1995 issue (#10) of *A New Direction*

"Freshman English for Church Leaders," published in the January 1995 issue (#9) of *A New Direction*

"Don't Like Us," published in the December 1994 issue of *Southern Forum*

"Gay Mormon History," book review of *Multiply and Replenish*, published in the November 1994 issue (#8) of *A New Direction*

"The Case Against Heterosexuality," published in the November 1994 issue (#8) of *A New Direction*

"*Born That Way?* An Irrelevant Answer to an Irrelevant Question," review of Erin Eldridge's book (1994 Deseret) in the September 1994 issue (#7) of *A New Direction*

"Family Values or Dirty Laundry?" published in the March 1994 issue (#33) of *Second Stone*

"Like It or Leave It," published in the March 1994 issue (#33) of *Second Stone*

"Can Gays Change?" published in the August 1993 issue (#43) of *Nomos*

"Gays and Lesbians Should Invade the Military," published in the July 28, 1993 issue of *Newsday*, and carried in *The Washington Post* and *The Los Angeles Times*

"Crossing Barriers of Race, Class, Gender, and Sexual
    Orientation," review of *A Certain Terror:
    Heterosexism, Militarism, Violence, and Change*,
    published in the July 1993 issue (#29) of *Second Stone*

"Should We Go Back?" published in the Spring 1993 issue
    (Vol. 22, #1) of *Common Sense*

"Red, White, and Blue Assumptions," published in the April
    1993 issue of *The Arizona Unconservative*

"Can Homophobia Be Cured?" review of the book by Bruce
    Hilton, published in the March 1993 issue (#27) of
    Second Stone

"Heterosexuals Are Not at Risk," published in the February
    1993 issue (Vol. 5, #1) of *Sexual Perspectives*

"The Exultant Misdiagnosis," published in the January 1993
    issue (#26) of *Second Stone*

"Out of the Bishop's Closet," review of the book by Antonio
    Feliz, published in the January 1993 issue (#26) of
    Second Stone

"Catholic Guilt," review of *Gay and Still Catholic: A Journey
    Home*, published in the November 1992 issue (#25) of
    Second Stone

"The Private Life of a Teacher," published in the May 1992
    issue (Vol. 56, #5) of *The Progressive*

"The Church's Circle of Sex," published in the March 1992
    issue (#4) of *A New Direction*

"The Ever-Changing Policies in the Mormon Church," published in the March 1992 issue (#4) of *A New Direction*

"Passion vs. Will: Homosexuality in Orson Scott Card's *Wyrms*," published in the August 1992 issue (#33) of *Riverside Quarterly*

"Peculiarly Good *Peculiar People*," published in the January 1992 issue (#20) of *Second Stone*

"Adam and Steve," published in the November 1991 issue (#19) of *Second Stone*

"Military Gays Deserve Legal Protection," published in the May 6, 1991 issue of *Newsday* and reprinted in the *Army Times* on Dec. 2, 1991

Short Stories

"Amen," published in the Winter 2017 issue (Vol. 50, No. 4) of *Dialogue: A Journal of Mormon Thought*

"The Girl from Treponema," published in *The Kindness of Strangers*, Wising Up Press: Decatur, GA, December 2016, eds. Charles Brockett and Heather Tosteson

"Life in the Dungeon," published in *Bad Jobs & Bullshit*, The Geeky Press: Indianapolis, August 2016, eds. Brad King, Amber Peckham, and Jessica Dyer.

"To Open the Eyes of the Blind," published in *Off the Rocks* vol. 19 (Jan 2016), ed. Allison Fradkin

"The Date," published in *Off the Rocks* vol. 18 (Dec 2014), ed. Allison Fradkin

"Life in the Dungeon," published in *Overtime*, #33, July 2014

"Playing the Card," published in *Off the Rocks* vol. 17 (Dec 2013), ed. Allison Fradkin

"The Mormon Victorian Society," published in the May 2013 issue (#4) of *Chelsea Station*

"The Golem of Rabbi Loew," published in *Queer Fish*, Pink Narcissus Press, eds. Rose Mambert and Margarita Bezdomnya, (Oct 2011)

"A Grain of Mustard Seed," published in *Off the Rocks* vol. 15, ed. Allison Fradkin (Sept 2011)

"A Life of Wind," published in issue #3 (Spring 2009) of *Drash*

"Pronouncing the Apostrophe," published in issue 71 (Summer 2009) of *Glimmer Train*

"Nanny Princess," winner of the 2007 *Sunstone* fiction contest and published in the December 2008 issue (#152) of *Sunstone*

"The Rift," published in the Autumn 2009 issue (Vol. L, #3) of *The Massachusetts Review*

"Transfer Cookies," published in issue 9:3-4 (2007) of *Harrington Gay Men's Literary Quarterly*

"The Buzzard Tree," published in the Winter 2007 issue of *Dialogue: A Journal of Mormon Thought*

"Electricity," published in September 1999 issue (#42) of
 Indulge

"Almond Milk," published in the anthology *In Our Lovely
 Deseret: Mormon Fictions*, Signature Books: Salt Lake
 City, 1998, ed. Robert Raleigh

"The Shepherd Boy," published in the December 1995 issue
 (#230) of *Christopher Street*

"Killing Babies," published in the Fall/Winter 1995/96 issue
 (Vol. 4, #1) of *Backspace*

"Tagging Along," published in the Summer 1995 issue (#3) of
 Gerbil

"Rapture," published in the Summer 1995 issue (Vol. 28, #2)
 of *Dialogue: A Journal of Mormon Thought*

"Bloodletting," published in the May 1995 issue (#225) of
 Christopher Street

"The Ditch," published in the December 1994 issue (#220) of
 Christopher Street

"The 9:20 Express Train to Hell," published in the Summer
 1994 issue (Vol. 2, #4) of *Backspace*

"Washing Dishes," published in the May 1994 issue (#213) of
 Christopher Street

"Moot," published in the Spring 1994 issue (Vol. 2, #3) of
 Backspace

"Coming Forces," published in the Winter 1993-94 issue (Vol.
 1, #9) of *Shockbox*

"The Pool Room," published in the Fall 1993 issue (Vol. 2, #1) of *Backspace*

"Returning Thanks," published in the June 1993 issue (Vol. 4, #41) of *The Ultimate Writer*

"Gifts," published in the Summer 1993 issue (Vol. 1, #4) of *Backspace*

"Mis ing Parts," published in the April 1993 issue (Vol. 12, #11) of *Words of Wisdom*

"Pissing in Peace," published in the May 1993 issue (#201) of *Christopher Street*

"Ronnie and Clyde," published in the Winter 1992-93 issue (#72) of *RFD*

"Out of Exile," published in the November and December 1992 issues (Vol. 7, #3 and #4) of *Bahlasti Papers*

"Crusades," published in the July 1992 issue of *Worm*

"Bus Surfing, U.S.A.," published in the March 1992 issue (#174) of *Christopher Street*

"The Odds," published in the Summer 1991 issue (#66) of *RFD*

"P-Day Man," published in the Summer 1991 issue (#66) of *RFD*

Talks

"The Banality of a Meaningful Contribution," presented for the Under the Rainbow storytelling group at the Edmunds Public Library, Feb 10, 2020

Presentation on the UpStairs Lounge fire given at the University of North Carolina—Wilmington, Oct 2012, as part of the Stonewall Lecture Series

"Chosen Family in Gay Mormon Literature," talk given at Sunstone symposium in Salt Lake in 2010

"Writing Literature, Not Tracts," talk given at Sunstone symposium in Salt Lake in 2009

Part of a panel discussion on the UpStairs Lounge fire on the 25th anniversary of the fire on June 24, 1998, at the U.S. Mint in New Orleans, along with Fire Chief William McCrossen, journalist Clancy DuBos, and survivor Courtney Craighead

"*The Crying Game*'s Tears—Misogyny or Masculinity?" presented at the American Society for Irish Studies conference in West Virginia in March 1994

"Mardi Gras Leather," seminar under the direction of Laurence Senelick at the American Society for Theatre Research conference in November 1993 in New Orleans

"Correctly Teaching Political Correctness," presented at the Louisiana Association for College Composition conference at Northeast Louisiana University in Monroe on October 4, 1991

Awards

Rainbow Awards 2017, Second Place for Best Gay Contemporary General Fiction: *The Last Days Linger*

Rainbow Awards 2015, Honorable Mention: *Gayrabian Nights*

Kirkus Reviews Best of 2015: *Missionaries Make the Best Companions* and *Despots of Deseret*

Kirkus Reviews Best of 2014: *Dragons of the Book of Mormon*

Kirkus Reviews Best of 2013: *The Mormon Victorian Society*

Kirkus Reviews Best of 2012: *Marginal Mormons*

Kirkus Reviews Best of 2011: *The Abominable Gayman*

Whitney Awards finalist 2007, Best Short LDS Fiction: "The Buzzard Tree"

CPSIA information can be obtained
at www.ICGtesting.com
Printed in the USA
BVHW071041250620
582308BV00001B/118